"Tamara Letter urges us all to become the '...best version of you that you can be' in her new book. She definitely possesses a super power and it's to help the children she teaches, the friends, colleagues, and family members she enlists, and the strangers she embraces to find within themselves a value for the ultimate gift we can give away—our kindness. *A Passion for Kindness* is a gift of kindness to all of us, especially educators who care deeply and want to help their students experience empathy for others. Throughout her book, Tamara also helps us see that planting seeds of kindness grows gardens, fields, and forests of care for others, especially those in pain, those with great loss, and those who feel hopeless. Her stories of RAK, also known as random acts of kindness, in response to the tragic loss of children's lives in school shootings at Sandy Hook Elementary and Marjory Stoneman Douglas High School help us all find rays of sunshine in these darkest of storms. Yes, Tamara certainly has a super power. Read her book—it will remind you that paying kindness forward doesn't cost us a dime, but it will result in an investment in a kinder future for our schools, communities, and world. Imagine a world filled with kindness—Tamara is making that happen!"

—**Pam Moran**, coauthor of *Timeless Learning* and executive director of the Virginia School Consortium for Learning

"Tamara Letter's book, *A Passion for Kindness*, is a must-have book for any kindness cultivator that wants to make the world a better place. Through her experiences, and the stories of those she spotlights, we are empowered with creative ways to show kindness to others. Her positivity shines throughout this book, reminding us that empathy, compassion, and connection can be found in everyone if we simply listen to the quiet whisper of our hearts."

—**Leon Logothetis**, best-selling author of *The Kindness Diaries*

"It can be tempting to dismiss a book like this as too feel-good, or even naive, in our current climate. But Tamara gives kindness a powerful voice and shows how simple acts can have lasting positive impacts. I loved every moment of reading this book and plan to revisit it often for its inspirational, yet practical, examples of kindness that can be implemented in school, home, and community. Tamara includes the research. Guess what? There is some truth to the power of this kindness stuff, folks, with goodness for both the giver and receiver. Don't just read this book: Put its lessons into practice, and together, with Tamara as our guide, we can overcome the negative forces that threaten to overwhelm us."

—**Karen Work Richardson**, PhD, executive director,
Virginia Society for Technology in Education

"I have been following Tamara's kindness journey on social media for a few years now and I am so grateful for this book where I can learn more about her incredible Passion Projects and the other ways Tamara instills kindness in every aspect of her life. In *A Passion for Kindness*, Tamara shares her insights, experiences, and ideas for how we can make the world a better place if only we cultivate kindness. As someone who believes in the power of social media for good, I fully appreciated each chapter's Kindness Cultivator, which celebrates a person in Tamara's life (online and in person) who is doing good in the world, for the world. This book will give you ideas for spreading positivity, no matter what subject or grade you teach. And let's face it, we can all use a little more kindness in the world."

—**Jennifer Casa-Todd**, teacher-librarian and
author of *Social LEADia*

"Tamara Letter gently folds in quotes, metaphors, stories, and points to ponder throughout her engaging book, *A Passion for Kindness*. The stories from Kindness Cultivators were just the examples needed as evidence of vulnerability, choices, seeing the unseen, knowing the power in roots and stems, and more. Tamara walks the reader through memories and some uncomfortable situations that led to random acts of kindness. She shares stories about how teachers empowered students to spread kindness throughout and beyond school. I highly recommend reading *A Passion for Kindness*. Just be aware that this book will touch your heart, change your thinking, and impact you so you will want to cultivate kindness. Thank you, Tamara!"

—**Barbara Bray**, creative learning strategist, author, blogger and podcast host at Rethinking Learning (barbarabray.net)

"Your heart will be filled with a passion for kindness and your head will be bursting with ideas after you read this engaging and inspiring book by Tamara Letter. Once you begin reading *A Passion for Kindness*, you will not want to put it down. Readers connect with Tamara through her own beautifully told stories of challenge and triumph while being absolutely in awe at her incredible devotion to spreading kindness everywhere. Being an avid kindness researcher, Tamara includes stories of others' kindness missions as well as a plethora of kindness resources. This book is not only a gift to all educators but to all of humankind. Tamara is a difference-maker and a world-changer and a blessing to us all as a transparent kindness ambassador."

—**Allyson Apsey**, elementary principal and author of *The Path to Serendipity*

"*A Passion for Kindness* is pure joy! Tamara had me captivated from beginning to end as she beautifully wove her own personal experiences with those of others to capture the incredible power of kindness. Each chapter is full of inspiring, practical ideas and thought-provoking questions to empower you to spread positivity and joy to those around you no matter who or where you serve. This book is a must-read that I highly recommend to anyone who wants to make this world a better place."

—**Tisha Richmond**, tech integration specialist and author of *Make Learning Magical*

"Tamara Letter takes you on an empathetic journey that will leave you inspired and compelled to sincere action. You will not only have a passion for kindness after reading, but you will be compelled to take sincere next steps to support others. Celebrate kindness and take these lessons to dynamic action for your community."

—**Sean Gaillard**, principal and author of *The Pepper Effect*

"In a world where kindness is often overlooked, Tamara Letter reminds us how even the smallest and simplest random acts of kindness can have an endless ripple effect on those near and far. From personal stories that relate to the heart to research and references that strengthen the mind, everyone who reads this book will be inspired to make the world a better place. We need more kindness in this world and Tamara will show you how you, and your students, can help."

—**Annick Rauch**, French immersion educator, learner, and mom

"Throughout the pages of *A Passion for Kindness*, Tamara Letter eloquently pens the stories of not only the acts of kindness she has personally shared with others, but those implemented by kindness cultivators around the world as well. As I read each carefully placed word within this beautiful work of art, I found myself saying, 'That's brilliant! I can do that! Why have I never considered that simple yet profound kind deed?'

"Tamara's storytelling moved me—deep within my soul. I'm not going to lie; sometimes it caused my eyes to leak a little. I was not only moved emotionally, but I was also moved to act! It's true: I now carry a roll of quarters with me everywhere I go.

"Do you want to make the world a better place? Every human (no matter your role in this thing called life) should read *A Passion for Kindness* and find ways to share more love to those around us."

—**Tara M. Martin**, educator, keynote speaker, and author of *Be REAL*

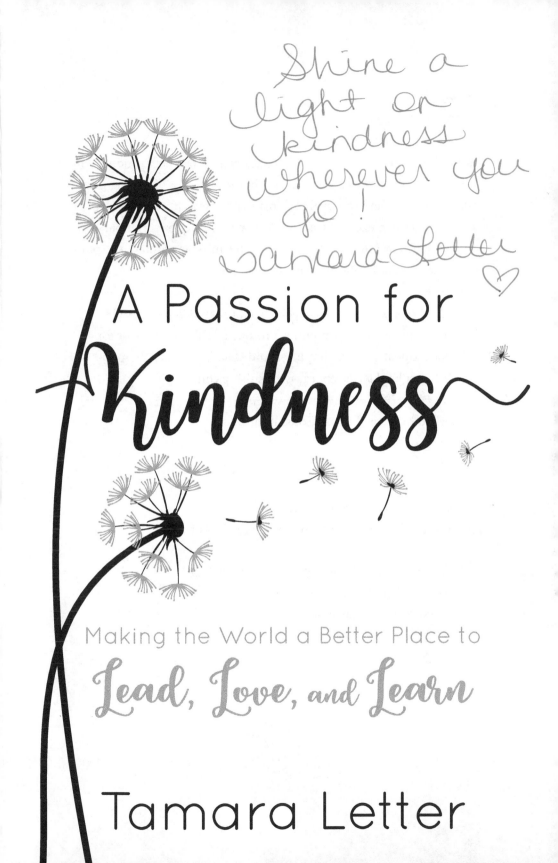

Shine a
light on
kindness
wherever you
go!
Tamara Letter ♡

A Passion for Kindness

Making the World a Better Place to
Lead, Love, and Learn

Tamara Letter

A Passion for Kindness
© 2019 by Tamara Letter

This book is available at special discounts when purchased in quantity for use as premiums, promotions, fundraisers, or for educational use. For inquiries and details, contact the publisher at books@daveburgessconsulting.com.

Published by Dave Burgess Consulting, Inc.
San Diego, CA
DaveBurgessConsulting.com

Cover Design by Genesis Kohler
Editing and Interior Design by My Writers' Connection

Library of Congress Control Number: 2019931205
Paperback ISBN: 978-1-949595-18-5
Ebook ISBN: 978-1-949595-19-2

First Printing: February 2019

Dedication

For Katrina, Daniel, and Caleb

Being chosen as your mom is the greatest gift
of kindness I could ever receive. Keep shining
your light for the world to see!

Contents

What Goes Around

When I was small, my grandmother had a favorite phrase she would repeat when she encountered others who were a bit unkind in their words or actions. "What comes around, goes around," she would mutter as she brushed off the negativity and went about her day. For years I viewed that phrase as one of vengeance, a punishment that would naturally occur to all those who had caused others hurt or pain. It wasn't until I was in my thirties that I realized the true power in those words—when viewed from the rose-colored glasses of optimism and positivity. What would happen if I shifted the perspective and chose to see the *good* that people did? Would that "come around" as well?

I believe each and every one of us has the power to make a positive impact on the world around us. As a cultivator of kindness, I have seen firsthand the boomerang effect: The joy you give others through your words and actions really does bounce back to you. Kindness inspires others to plant their own seeds, which take root and bloom in remarkable ways. The process continues in countless ways, even without our knowledge.

The beauty of kindness is that it's not a tale of him or her or even you or me. It's a journey *we* share together. We do not live in silos from morning to night. Each day we are called to work with others, to coexist in a world where kindness is rarely a black-and-white task listed on our daily agendas. We have to be intentional about it and prioritize kindness by setting the example ourselves.

We can be the good.

We can spark the light.

We can be a catalyst of change.

We can make a positive difference in this world.

The lessons learned and shared in this book are universal; they apply at school, at home, in the workplace, and in our travels. How we treat others is about valuing human potential; with kindness, the world is a little brighter, a little easier, a bit more manageable. We are reminded that we are never truly alone.

Quite simply, kindness matters.

As you turn the pages, you will learn more about my personal kindness journey and encounter stories of kindness cultivators around the world who are making a difference in their classrooms and communities. From a group called Secret Sisters who commit acts of kindness for grieving families to educators across the world joining together to flash mob kindness on an inner-city pizzeria, you will be inspired to lead, love, and learn.

In the chapters ahead, you will dive deep to sit with elementary students who are creating kindness passion projects and discover high school students who are using their talents to change communities one nail at a time. You will explore school-wide kindness initiatives and the multitude of ways to start a cultural shift focused on empathy and compassion.

This book will introduce you to students, teachers, and school leaders who believe in the power of altruism, showcasing methods of working together to make this world a better place. You can even learn more about kindness organizations and explore free resources to enhance your classroom lessons and school programs.

Even if you are not an educator by profession, the stories shared in this book can be applied to your life. Challenge yourself to reflect on the Points to Ponder at the end of each chapter and seek out new opportunities to shine a light on inspiration.

If you are looking for simple ways to positively impact others, this is the book for you!

Kindness inspires.

Be the good!

Section
1

Seeds of Inspiration

If I cannot do great things, I can do small things in a great way.

—Martin Luther King, Jr.

Chapter 1

The Power of Words

Kind words can be short
and easy to speak,
but their echoes are
truly endless.

—Mother Teresa

"Has anyone ever been the new kid in town? Anyone move in the middle of a school year? What was that like for you?"

I posed that question to a class of fifth graders, who immediately raised their hands and voices, eager to share stories of feeling awkward and uncomfortable, of being afraid, embarrassed, and humiliated. But not one student shared a story of kindness.

I dug a little deeper with my questioning. "What was it like that first day? What do you remember?"

More stories of fear and nervousness, wanting to cry, feeling the glare of others staring back at you. Still no kindness.

Eventually a soft-spoken girl raised her hand to speak.

"The first day was hard, but my teacher was really nice to me."

Other students turned to face her, and I breathed a sigh of relief.

Finally. Something positive.

Once she shared her experience, another girl chimed in with a happy memory, then another, and another, and another. All of a sudden, this class that, moments before, was knee-deep in sorrow and despair had sailed into a calmer sea of fond reflections. Unfortunately, we still had one glaring problem before us, the elephant in the room.

Many of these students were not being kind to one another.

I brought them together to share my own personal story of being the new kid in town. I wanted them to see the power of their words and how words spoken at the age of ten could still resonate in the heart of an adult decades later. This is where my kindness story begins.

The Picked-On Kid

I was the picked-on kid. Short. Freckles. Glasses. A recipe for social disaster when you're the new kid in town. We had moved only ten miles east, but you would have thought we landed in a new world. Everything was different.

New house. New school. New rules.

It was the middle of my third-grade year, and all I saw was loss. Before my mom could finish packing my metal Strawberry Shortcake lunchbox, I knew my first day would be a disaster. I didn't want to leave the friends I knew so well. I didn't want a new beginning, and I was filled with conflicting emotions that I couldn't describe. Everything felt out of control.

My panic rose as I walked through the unfamiliar hallways on that first day in my new school. What if I entered the wrong classroom? What if nobody played with me at recess? What if I had to go to the bathroom? What if I got on the wrong bus to go home? I was consumed with worry and wanted to run away, but there was nothing I could do to relieve the fear. I had to enter the classroom and find my seat.

That's when I heard the whispers.

"She's the new kid."

"Where did she come from?"

"What's her name again? Tammy . . . PAYNE?"

"Oh yeah, I bet she is a pain, too. You can already tell."

"Her glasses look like Coke bottles."

I had barely taken off my coat when the cruel words filled my ears. It was the first time I realized my last name was a homophone. Their careless comments reddened my cheeks as I slid farther down in my seat, the fear and embarrassment immobilizing any attempt at unpacking my supplies.

I was the new kid in class, and they already hated me.

I paused my story, the past fading into present day as I looked at the fifth graders sitting there. The silence in the room was deafening. Some students fiddled with their fingers in their laps. Some looked away when my eyes met theirs. Everyone felt the weight of my words.

"That happened to me when I was eight years old. I am now in my forties, and I can still hear their taunts in my mind as if it was yesterday. I am sharing this story with you for one reason alone: Your. Words. Matter. Choose them wisely, for they will last longer than the notebooks you are writing in today."

When students were given an opportunity to share their voices by completing an online survey on friendship, they poured their hearts out on the final question: "What do I want my teacher to know?"

Their responses revealed who was being excluded and why, who got into an argument with a friend, and who was not playing fairly at recess. When given a chance to share their voices, it was clear who was being kind and who was not. It was time to readjust my lessons. I needed to provide some intentional grouping with a variety of activities that provided more opportunities for communication and collaboration. I had to reflect on the words I used with students. *Did they lift others up or tear them apart? How did my responses translate back to them?* These insights into my own behavior reminded me, yet again, of the power of words.

The Social Dilemma

Social dynamics in the classroom can make or break your year. Students spend at least six hours a day in the confines of a classroom or a school, and during that time they are expected to master the curriculum taught while also navigating the tumultuous waters of social interaction. Are we guiding them in the power of their words as they do this?

How do we approach students who are being unkind with their words? Is it their issue or one we pass along to the school counselor, assuming they will be able to fix the problem? Do we interrupt them halfway through their comment in class, with no alternative way for them to share their thoughts with others? What is our role in shaping students as they converse with their classmates?

Every person in the school community has a stake in the game of guiding students to be respectful, productive citizens. We can't turn away and assume someone else will deal with the issues that arise. When we sign that contract each year to continue our journey as educators, we commit to teaching students not only the state-mandated curriculum but also the unspoken nuances of working together, building relationships, and growing into adults who can harness their own potential to make their mark in this world.

What opportunities are we providing students to practice these skills in class? Are we teaching them to be aware of the weight of their words?

It starts with us.

In Chapter 5 of *Shift This!: How to Implement Gradual Changes for MASSIVE Impact in Your Classroom*, Joy Kirr provides practical examples of how to shift discussions in the classroom so that students are empowered to share their voices:

- **Whole-group Discussions:** All students respond to one question with a limited number of answers, splitting the room into halves or fourths, then take turns to share their perspectives in a respectful way.
- **Fishbowl Discussions:** A small group of students sit in the center of the room with remaining classmates spanning out in circles behind to act as observers or recorders until they want to join in the conversation.
- **Backchannel Discussions:** Students add their thoughts to a discussion digitally without speaking aloud.
- **EdCafes:** Questions are placed around the room to prompt small group discussions based on interest or preference.
- **Harkness Method:** Students sit around a table and discuss questions about their current topic of study.[1]

Whether you implement traditional modes of communication such as speaking face-to-face or choose to demonstrate the power of technological tools such as Google Apps, Flipgrid, or Seesaw, student voice is essential to creating a kind culture in and out of the classroom. It's imperative to provide a safe place where students can practice digital communication before they engage in real-time online banter, which can have life-changing consequences if used inappropriately.

Kind words are evident in our day-to-day lives. The challenge is recognizing those moments when they occur. Starbucks employees ask for your name so when your order is ready, it's a more personable experience than just shouting out, "Who ordered the tall, skinny, nonfat, mocha latte?" Chick-fil-A employees complete every action with, "My pleasure." These simple statements are small, yet powerful, ways to make someone's day a little brighter.

Whether you are an educator, business owner, parent, or coworker, the same principles apply.

Your. Words. Matter.

To boost the impact of your message, reflect on the words you use with others on a regular basis: in conversations, during meetings, in the classroom, with your family. Do your words make people smile? Do they encourage positive interaction? How do you use your words to inspire others?

What I experienced as the picked-on kid sparked a desire to help similar children overcome hurdles to reach their highest potential. It is the earliest memory I have of wanting to be a teacher in order to make a difference in the lives of others. What I couldn't foresee at that time was the role kindness would play in that journey.

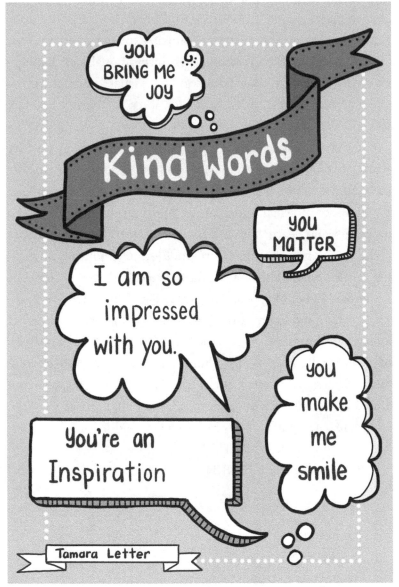

Illustration: Julie Woodard (@woodard_julie)

Choose Kind

Each time Theresa Holloran's prekindergarten students enter her classroom, they tap a "Choose Kind" sign taped outside her door. In a tweet she posted to Twitter, Holloran explained:

Just as football players touch an inspirational sign before a game, my students touch #choosekind . . . a visual reminder, a physical reminder to treat others with kindness (@TheresaHolloran, July 23, 2018).

Her students are learning important lessons about positive social interaction with their peers and other adults even before they can read and write.

Think of the small moments in your morning. Do they set a tone of joy and peace? Tara Martin (@TaraMartinEDU), author of *Be REAL: Educate from the Heart*, finds joy in the journey by making her first email of the day a gratitude email, thanking someone she knows. In her blog post, "Gratitude First," she states:

"I want my thoughts to be authentic, so I'm constantly on the lookout for things for which to be thankful. As I see them or think of them, I make a note on my phone, type a text to myself, or voice memo a message so I can listen to it later."[2] Choosing words of gratitude to share with others brings joy to both parties!

There is a popular display in classrooms and schools across the country using the acronym THINK:

Before you speak, THINK!

Is it:

    T–True

    H–Helpful

    I–Inspiring

    N–Necessary

    K–Kind

Illustration: Julie Woodard
(@woodard_julie)

Another popular adage is "Pause Before You Post," which conveys the importance of taking time to think about our digital communication before we share it with the world. We all can use these reminders from time to time! Embracing the power of words is choosing words in deliberate ways to uplift, not tear down. It's one of the many free ways to show kindness to the world!

Negate the Naysayers

Recognizing the impact of our words is not limited to students and teachers in the classroom. Each person you know has the power of words at their disposal. Do your words heal or harm? One of my dear friends, Annick Rauch (@AnnickRauch), a first-grade French immersion teacher in Winnipeg, Manitoba, Canada, reminds me, "Stepping on others doesn't make you taller." She's absolutely right! Pushing down people to shine a light on yourself only dims the view others see.

In *Shame Nation: The Global Epidemic of Online Hate*, Sue Scheff and Melissa Schorr tackle the discussion of digital communication, hate shaming, and online bullying with vivid examples and heartbreaking stories. They emphasize the importance of understanding the limitations of free speech:

Not everything you say or type online is appropriate or allowed. ... Defamation is not condoned as part of free speech. Opinions or satire are one thing, but if you're presenting something that's incorrect and damaging to an individual's reputation as if it's a statement of fact, it may land you in legal trouble.[3]

These are lessons we all need to know. Whether it's a haphazard tweet or a ranting response on a blog post, we need to pause before we post. Spewing negativity with the intent to cause others harm or creating a virtual mob of hate only fans the flames of wildfire that at any given moment can switch directions and burn right back to the one who struck the match.

What you post online becomes the public's perception of you. While some might counter their posts with a nonchalant, "I was just kidding around," the world makes a snap judgment of your worth within mere seconds of an online post. Not only can the world access what you post, it can see what you like and comment on as well, thanks to complex social media algorithms that control what shows up in your feeds. No digital platform is immune to the damaging power of a negative screenshot. Our social media feeds are quickly becoming an autobiographical résumé, which is a lesson our students must hear from multiple people.

My role as a technology integrator and instructional coach with Hanover County Public Schools in Mechanicsville, Virginia, is to support teachers as they use technology in the classroom for instructional purposes. My role also includes providing professional development to teachers, administrators, and other leaders throughout our district in the use of technology for a variety of purposes. I constantly remind children and adults about the importance of negating the naysayers with positivity.

Danny Steele, principal and co-author of *Essential Truths for Educators* and *Essential Truths for Principals* with Todd Whitaker (@ToddWhitaker), inspires me daily with his encouraging posts on social media. Whether he's sharing his experiences as an administrator or describing small moments that bring him joy, I am always uplifted. His perspective on positive posts reflects my beliefs as well:

The educators who are constantly tweeting positivity are not in denial about the very real challenges that educators face. They just realize that a good attitude gives you the best chance of solving those problems, and they understand that a negative outlook destroys motivation (@SteeleThoughts, June 6, 2018).

It's true that you won't get along with everyone you meet, but you can still be kind to unkind people. While it's hard to build a bridge of trust with someone when the flames of anger burn beneath, try anyway. If you have an issue with a comment or response someone shared, speak to them in private or send a message directly. Don't rant and rave as a public power play. There's a thin line between civility with respectable discussions and rude, judgmental responses, both applicable to online and offline behavior.

Find the people in your world who will lift you up and help you soar. Seek out the joy ambassadors and kindness cultivators who remind you that there is good in the world. Develop your own network of positivity and let your light shine! It takes perseverance to show kindness in all situations. It takes courage to stand by those who are being knocked down by others. Embrace the knowledge that we are all works in progress and remember that even one step forward is a step in the right direction.

Kindness Cultivator Spotlight

Akilah Ellison

#JoyAmbassadors and #VBHasJoy

Twitter: @OrganicLeaderVB

Website: joyisrevolutionary.blogspot.com

Akilah Ellison, a middle school administrator with Virginia Beach City Public Schools, understands the importance of creating positive culture in classrooms and schools. Recognizing the fluctuation of morale throughout the school year, she proposed a new program to district leaders that would identify select educators as Joy Ambassadors in each school. The idea was these educators would provide year-round support to increase joy throughout the district.

In 2016, more than 147 teachers across eighty-four schools in the district had designated Joy Ambassadors in their buildings. These teachers attend meetings throughout the year to cultivate kindness, joy, and mindfulness in others. Their focus includes two key areas—student learning environments and teacher well-being.

"Teachers can't serve from an empty vessel," Akilah explains. "We tell them that to do the best for every child and for every child to feel valued and loved, it takes a teacher feeling empowered and inspired."

Using monthly newsletters, Akilah and other Joy Ambassadors provide additional resources to maintain momentum year-round.

Joy Ambassadors share their experiences on social media using the hashtags #JoyAmbassadors and #VBHasJoy, spotlighting the many ways they bring happiness back into their work. From bowling nights and inspirational poster-making to transforming campus spaces into Joy Rooms, they share ideas, celebrate milestones, and actively search for ways to keep joy a focus in all they do. They even host an annual Joy Fair with multiple stations including a photo booth, wellness demonstrations, and Joy Jar creations.

To learn more about Akilah Ellison's passion for kindness, favorite kindness quotes, and more, visit tamaraletter.com.

Points to Ponder

 Are you showing kindness to yourself? What words are you using to describe yourself when you peer into the mirror?

Think about the people in your inner circle: friends, family, coworkers. Are they using words that inspire or tear down? How can you create a cultural shift to emphasize positivity?

What are three simple phrases you can say to someone else to brighten their day?

Chapter 2

40 RAKs

> A journey of a
> thousand miles
> begins with a
> single step.
>
> —Lao Tzu

We sat together on the sofa brainstorming ways to celebrate my upcoming birthday, the big 4-0. My forever friend, Lisa, laughed at the outrageous list she had created, from traveling the world in seven days to skydiving over the sea. All I could do was shake my head.

"I want to do something simple," I told her. "Meaningful. Nice. Something different."

We pondered a bit more, the pencil lines smudging our papers as we erased, rewrote, and started again. It was the summer of 2012, and I had recently become a Pinterest convert, so I pulled up the website and scrolled through the stream of pins from others in my network.

As I typed "fortieth birthday ideas" into the search bar, a photograph on the page caught my attention. It was a woman wearing a birthday hat and holding a cup of coffee in her hand, and the photo caption jumping off the page: "34 acts of kindness for my 34th birthday!" I clicked on the image, which redirected me to a website where this woman described the acts of kindness she had completed for her birthday. Most were simple gestures, holding the door for someone else or smiling at five people throughout the day. A few were more elaborate like making dinner for a neighbor. I glanced up from my laptop to see Lisa staring back at me, her intuition kicking into high gear as she saw the sparkle in my eye.

In an instant my life changed forever.

Finding Purpose

As I teetered on the edge of that milestone birthday, I believed I had reached my potential for all things good and true. I was a mom to three great children and an educator with an advanced degree. I sang in the church choir and helped others in need. I considered myself to be a nice, well-rounded person who worked hard to do the right thing. But to do something that would have a global impact, to lead and inspire complete strangers? Now that was going a little over the top. My adulthood was a comfortable status-quo, paint-by-numbers canvas where everything had order and symmetry.

It was time to pick up the brush and paint outside the lines.

Celebrating Kindness

Celebrations are an integral part of communities around the world, especially for milestone events such as birthdays, religious holidays, and independence remembrances. They are woven through our cultural tapestries as fine threads, their shimmer and shine illuminating moments of brilliance that draw us out of our normal day-to-day experiences. Celebrations bring joy and camaraderie, a communal experience for all involved.

But celebrating kindness? Who does that?

Apparently, me.

That night a seed of inspiration was planted deep in my soul. I didn't know it at the time, but I had just embarked on a journey that would transform every aspect of my life as a teacher, a mom, a daughter, and a friend. I had discovered my divine purpose: to celebrate kindness in every way possible.

Getting Started

Sometimes the hardest part of getting started is getting started. I grabbed a sheet of paper and numbered it one to forty. I jotted down notes on potential acts of kindness I could do for others. Write a thank you note. Pay a stranger a compliment. Give someone flowers. As the paper filled with ideas, I quickly realized a list was unnecessary. I didn't want this birthday celebration to be scripted like a play, and I didn't feel the need to complete all forty acts in a twenty-four-hour time period. My plan was to take it day by day, see what happened, and allow kindness to flow when the opportunity was right.

Whew! One hurdle done! My next dilemma was how to document my stories of kindness. I envisioned a leisurely walk through my local bookstore, the leather-bound journals whispering, "Write in me!" Like many educators, I have a mild obsession with school supplies, so the thought of journaling with my favorite ultra-fine Sharpie made me giddy from the start.

"You need a website!" Lisa shouted from across the room, pulling me away from my thoughts. "A blog! You should start a blog!"

Going Digital

A blog? I had no clue what a blog was, much less how to make one. I had to search Google just to define the word! After a half-hour of reading various articles closing the gap of my limited knowledge, I realized Lisa was right. If I wanted to share my stories with others, I would need a digital platform.

I chose WordPress as my blogging website, and with a few taps on the keyboard, I had a customized URL website, ready to go. How exciting!

Actually, that's a bit of an exaggeration. While there was an immediate rush of exhilaration at the thought that someone else might read something I wrote, it was quickly diminished by the fear of what that really meant. Even before I had completed my first act of kindness, I was already worried about what others would think. What if my stories were boring? What if I published something with a typo and everyone judged me? Oh, the irony that a teacher can't spell! What if someone ridiculed me in the comments section or, even worse, shared my blog on Facebook with hideous heckling? Could I withstand the negativity? Would I feel like a picked-on eight-year-old again?

Overcoming Fear

Friends, let me tell you, fear is a paralyzing emotion. It wraps you in a straitjacket, keeping you immobile, whispering lies inside your head.

Don't listen to the lies.

You are bound for greatness! Your words and actions contain such power to inspire others, even in the simplest ways. Find a way to battle the dragons and slay the enemy, then get back up and continue moving forward. Remember what fear represents:

False

Evidence

Appearing

Real

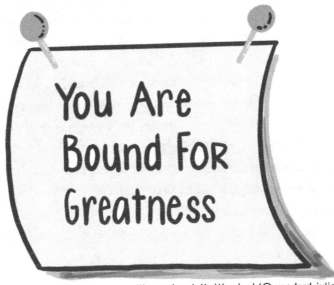

You Are Bound For Greatness

Illustration: Julie Woodard (@woodard_julie)

The world needs to hear your words.

The world needs to see your actions.

The world needs *you*!

Overcome fear by ignoring the lies. Regain your focus. Remind yourself of your purpose. Push the fear aside and shift "What if?" to "Why not?" Recognize the cadence of positivity in your heart and let it beat for all it's worth.

If you are struggling with the fear of getting started, you're not alone! Making that first move is the scariest part. Remember the words of Nelson Mandela, "I learned that courage was not the absence of fear, but the triumph over it. . . . The brave man is not he who does not feel afraid, but he who conquers that fear."[1]

You must conquer fear to move forward.

Taking the First Step

The process of creating my blog, which had seemed too overwhelming to imagine, was actually quite simple. After logging into WordPress, I scanned the available design templates and chose a preset option. The fonts, colors, and background images were already selected, making it even easier to take the first step.

I named the blog for my passion: *Celebrate Kindness*. I typed an overview of my fortieth birthday project on the main page and spent the rest of my evening exploring settings and customizing options. Personalizing the blog gave me more control and ownership, minimizing my fear. I reminded myself that though my blog was accessible, the link hadn't been shared with anyone so the risk of messing it up was minimal.

I didn't have any stories ready to write, as my *Celebrate Kindness* project was still evolving, so I opened a Google Doc to transform my handwritten kindness brainstorming into a digital plan of action. My goal was to document forty random acts of kindness (RAKs for short), one for each year of my life, then showcase the stories with words and pictures.

Lisa, a public relations specialist turned professional photographer, urged me to take a headshot and create business cards to pass out to others. "How else will people know where to read your story? You have to direct people to your website." I took her advice, created a stack of cards I could distribute to others, and waited for the perfect time to begin.

Embracing Opportunity

When we begin a new endeavor, we often seek perfection from the start without realizing the beauty in spontaneity. As a self-professed planner, I had it all mapped out. I would start my acts of kindness on my birthday in September and complete three to four acts of kindness each month. That pace would give me enough time to document each moment, publish, and share.

Satisfied with my perfect plan of kindness, I put the project aside as I enjoyed the lazy days of summer break. One July evening, as I was standing in a checkout line at our local grocery store, there was a delay with the woman in front of me processing her payment. I overheard the cashier inform her that her credit card was denied and that she needed another form of payment. The woman shifted the child on her hip to look inside her purse, presumably for another card or cash, but came up empty-handed. The cashier started to clear away the bagged groceries, and my heart simply broke at the thought of this woman not having what she needed to feed the child she was carrying.

I took a breath and entered their conversation, leaning forward and handing my credit card to the cashier. "Ma'am, just add those things to my groceries. I'll buy your dinner tonight." Both women looked at me with surprise, with the one ahead of me immediately refusing my offer, but I stated it again, with determination. She accepted, thanking me profusely for the help.

I slid my credit card into the machine then scrawled my website address on the back of the receipt. I briefly explained about my fortieth birthday project and asked her permission to share her story. Because I hadn't planned to start my project for another two months, it hadn't occurred to me to carry my new cards with me! I could hear Lisa's voice ringing in my ears: "How will people find the stories you write if you don't share your website link with them?"

After leaving the store, I returned to my car and sat for a while before heading home. My thoughts were spinning. *This was the moment! This was the opportunity to start my Forty RAKs for Forty Years!* Laughing out loud at the irony, I realized I had spent so much time planning the RAKs that I had forgotten what the R represented—*random*.

Yes, that first act of kindness cost me a little bit of money that I hadn't expected to spend, but it was the right thing to do. I empathized with her plight and shared the feeling of embarrassment when her credit card was denied. It was the first time I had ever entered a stranger's conversation so boldly and the first time I had paid for a stranger's groceries. It became the first stop on my journey to celebrate kindness.

40 RAKs

From that moment, my eyes were opened to opportunities for kindness. Sometimes, like the day I donated flowers and games to an assisted living facility in honor of a relative's birthday, I had a plan of action for blessing someone else. Other times, like the day my daughter and I were caught in a downpour at an amusement park and shared our umbrella with a stranger, I was simply in the right place at the right time.

Most of the forty RAKs were low-cost or free: buying a stranger's coffee at Starbucks, overpaying my toll to cover the person behind me on the interstate, writing thank you notes, picking up litter, and baking cookies for firemen. I even donated some of my treasured children's books to a Little Free Library in town.

To learn more about the Little Free Library, visit littlefreelibrary.org.

As the acts of kindness continued, so did my blogging journey. I was writing and publishing, trying to overcome the fear of imperfection, recognizing the story was more important than my revisions. My hope was that the RAK recipients would visit my website, read the stories, and be inspired to do the same for someone else.

I wasn't seeking attention or fame and was reluctant to promote the project on social media. I had an ongoing fear that people would misunderstand my purpose, thinking the kind acts were a gimmick or promotion. Countless times I would read posts chastising those who had shared openly about their kind acts. Comments such as "You shouldn't seek attention for being nice" or "I don't need to tell the world about things I do" made me even more hesitant to share my RAKs.

But I truly believed sharing my project would benefit others. I knew that sharing stories about kindness could inspire others to see the world around them in a different way. While there is nothing wrong with doing kind actions in private, without acknowledgment or attention, it doesn't mean that's the only acceptable way to spread kindness. Imagine if no one ever spoke of gifts given or received. How would we be inspired to do the same in other circumstances?

I finally decided to take the plunge and share my stories on Facebook. Although my Facebook feed only consisted of people I knew in person, it was still nerve-wracking. The fear of failure, criticism, and ridicule was ever-present, but my passion for kindness was stronger. I posted my stories and tagged a few of my closest friends, knowing their support would bolster any negativity I might encounter.

You know what happened next? Nobody posted a negative comment. No one made a snarky comment about my grammar or spelling. Every like and comment let me know that others were reading my story and engaging in my kindness journey. Their kind words gave me the confidence to share again. And again. And again.

Remember that your story is important and worth sharing. Be brave! We are better together! Even if you face criticism along the way, those moments will be few and far between. Don't let the "what ifs" destroy you! Push away the barrage of fear that blocks your mind. In *Teach Like a Pirate*, Dave Burgess (@burgessdave) addresses the most common reasons people falter at the starting line or don't start at all:

1. Fear of failure
2. Believing you have to figure it all out before you begin
3. Perfectionism
4. Lack of focus
5. Fear of criticism or ridicule[2]

If you have experienced any of these, you are not alone! Each was a hurdle I had to clear to make my fortieth birthday project come to fruition, and they constantly appear in other aspects of my life. We must recognize our roadblocks and find ways to forge ahead. Our purpose is worth it!

Kindness Cultivator Spotlight

Roman Nowak

#bekindEDU

Twitter: @NowakRo

Instagram: roman.nowak

Website: mrromannowak.wordpress.com

Roman Nowak, a high school language arts teacher at École secondaire catholique L'Escale in Rockland, Ontario, Canada, shares his passion for kindness across a variety of social media platforms, including Twitter and Instagram. "I have always been a spiritual and religious person," he says. "My parents brought me up in a very religious setting, but most importantly, they were always examples of how important it was to do things for others." This inspiration of generosity continues today as Roman shares his enthusiasm for kindness with his wife and two daughters. From raising funds for cancer research to organizing runs and Christmas food drives, kindness is a constant focus in his world.

In conversations with his friend Eli Casaus (@MrCoachEli), the two created an online kindness community using the hashtag #bekindEDU, posting daily messages of positivity, hope, empathy, and compassion. In 2018, the duo created a weekly Twitter chat using the same hashtag to connect like-minded kindness cultivators and provide a space for sharing ideas, sparking additional kind acts across the globe.

While emphasizing the power of small moments of kindness, Roman has been surprised by kind acts in return.

Brandi Miller (@bmilla84), a first-grade teacher at Caldwell Elementary School in Florida, has sent small "smile packages" from her students to brighten his day. One package included a class *Book of Kindness* her students wrote and dedicated to him, following the work they had shared together. "I have that book on my desk and cherish it. It meant the world to me."

To learn more about Roman Nowak's passion for kindness, favorite kindness quotes, and more, visit tamaraletter.com.

Points to Ponder

- ✻ What conversations have you shared with someone else that created a spark of inspiration? How did you transform those ideas into action?

- ✻ Think of a time you stepped out of your comfort zone to try something new. What pushed you to keep going?

- ✻ Have you encountered naysayers along your journey? How do you combat the negativity?

Chapter 3

RAKs for Sandy Hook

Do what you can,
with what you've
got, where you are.

—Theodore Roosevelt

Making intentional choices to bless others with kindness shifted many aspects of my life. It was as if my eyes had been closed but were suddenly opened. Things appeared a little brighter, and there was a spirit of purpose wrapped around my day. Instead of crowds of strangers rushing past, I saw individual people, all unique and beautiful in their own ways. I caught myself slowing my pace to soak up these interactions, my jubilation shared with each RAK I completed.

As I continued to celebrate kindness, my family and friends took notice and showered me with kindness as well. A coworker sent me a gift card to a hair salon, saying I could pay it forward to surprise a stranger. A friend mailed me a check for twenty dollars, wanting to join in the fun but unsure how to go about it. Parents provided books to donate to daycare centers, and students offered toys and stuffed animals to those who had none. The more stories I shared, the more people offered to help. Kindness was spreading in ways I never imagined!

The Impact of Tragedy

Amid all that joy, my world came to a crashing halt. On December 14, 2012, as I was sharing my thirty-eighth random act of kindness, I learned of the shooting at Sandy Hook Elementary School in Newtown, Connecticut. The horror of that day is burned into my memory like a heated cattle prod. My bubble of kindness burst with sorrow and grief.

I was devastated. Distraught. Paralyzed. Overwhelmed. Inconsolable. I couldn't wrap my mind around an armed shooter entering an elementary school with the intent to kill students and staff. It was unfathomable. Although I lived states away, it was as if the shooting had happened in my own community. The news media replayed the scenes so often, I had to turn off the TV and disconnect from social media. My heart simply broke in two.

It was a struggle to finish out the last two acts of kindness for my blog, to stay positive, and to act as if life were normal. As Christmas approached and I sat with my own three children, their beautiful lives untouched from the terror in this world, I wanted to wrap them in a cocoon and protect them forever. I was overwhelmed by guilt, watching my children open their presents while other families stared at unwrapped gifts under the tree.

I was frightened and felt completely helpless in the face of a tragedy that shook our profession to the core. I wanted to do something, anything, to help my educational community heal and find a way to regain our footing.

As I searched online for kindness ideas, I came across an article that listed the names of all the victims of the Sandy Hook tragedy with photos and brief descriptions. As these precious faces stared back at me, I knew that *Celebrate Kindness* had a larger purpose.

It was to recognize the good in humanity.

It was to shine a light on positivity and pave the way for others to do the same.

It was to remember the names of every life lost that day.

In January 2013, I extended my *Celebrate Kindness* project to include #26acts, a movement started by Ann Curry, former anchor of *The Today Show* on NBC. Her call to action was straightforward: complete an act of kindness in remembrance of lives lost at Sandy Hook Elementary School and share your story through social media using the hashtag #26acts. I decided that doing one act of kindness wasn't enough. I wanted to do one for each life lost that day.

My first act of kindness for #26acts was in memory of six-year-old Noah Pozner. I bought six smiley-face balloons and tied them to the fence at our local playground with a sign that said, "Free Balloons! Take One!" A note attached to each balloon, with a quarter to act as a weight, explained that the free balloon was an act of kindness in memory of Noah. I encouraged whoever took the balloon to read my blog post and leave a comment. By the time I returned to my car, two balloons had already been taken.

The next day, I discovered a new comment on my blog from a woman named Jennifer, explaining the impact my act of kindness had on her son, Eli, who has autism. She described her son's delight in the free balloon and shared examples of why that balloon meant so much to her child. "He had kept it in his closet because he was cherishing the balloon and didn't want to lose it. … I make the promise to you that I will pay it forward and keep Noah's memory

alive."[1] Her words gave me goosebumps as I realized the ripple effect had already begun.

I shared my post on Twitter with the hashtag #26acts and tagged Ann Curry (@AnnCurry) in a moment of risk-taking. Once again, I felt that twinge of fear, of someone mistaking my purpose in sharing my act of kindness. I wasn't doing this for attention. I truly believed then, as I do now, that words and actions have the power to make a difference in the lives of others.

We simply must be brave enough to share.

That tweet gave me a taste of what it's like to "go viral," as Ann Curry retweeted it to her followers. My blog post received more than 500 views that day with several hundred more throughout the week. While this is nothing close to the millions of views a viral video might receive now, it was a grand introduction to the power of social media and the importance of sharing our experiences globally. As Jennifer Casa-Todd (@JCasaTodd) emphasizes in *Social LEADia: Moving Students from Digital Citizenship to Digital Leadership*, "the more positive behaviors ... we can find and model, both online and offline, the better off everyone will be."[2]

Change in Operations

The tragedy at Sandy Hook Elementary School resulted in an immediate change in operations for our school and others around the country. We suddenly had armed officers monitoring the hallways of our open campus. Extra security was put into place with scannable badges and doorbells for locked buildings. There was an increased emphasis on visitors signing in and wearing name tags at all times. The level of access became more controlled with additional safety drills mandated to provide practice in high-alert situations.

While the mass shootings at Sandy Hook Elementary, Columbine High School, and Virginia Tech reminded educators and parents to be vigilant, the tragedies also affected communities and businesses. Some companies rewrote their policy and procedure manuals to include redesigning entryways with reinforced doors, no longer allowing doors to be propped open, and requiring the last person leaving the building to notify security.

After Sandy Hook, we faced a new dilemma: How do we live, work, and play in a world of violence and tragedy, while continuing to create a warm, kind, and caring community?

We make kindness a priority.

The Messages We Send

Being kind to others does not mean you are naive or a pushover. You can be firm but polite in your words and actions. Having a passion for kindness means you acknowledge constraints and still find a way to be the good.

Every interaction we have with a student, staff member, parent, or stakeholder is an opportunity to show kindness and make a positive impact. We can even show kindness in our procedures by taking a closer look at the underlying messages we send in our workplaces and communities.

In his blog post titled "Same Message, Different Delivery," George Couros (@gcouros) shared his experience with workplace signs that send conflicting messages despite their intent. When entering a school building with a colleague, he counted the number of times he saw negative words displayed such as "no," "stop," or "don't." (One school had about seven before they even made it to the classroom!) His post spotlighted the underlying negativity sometimes displayed through words, fonts, and graphics.[3]

What are the hidden messages shown in the signs around your workplace or community? Do they promote a culture of welcome and acceptance or evoke emotions of control, fear, or apprehension?

We must be intentional about our words and actions, but we need to be cognizant of how they are received. Body language, tone, and word choice all contribute to the messages we send in person. Text-only messages remove two of the three, thus placing more emphasis on the words themselves. When choosing our words, we must also consider purpose, location, context, and recipient. Are we using our words to promote a culture of positivity and acceptance?

One way we can do this is to find small ways to encourage a positive culture. Perhaps you can create a compliment station near your copier, filled with blank notecards and colorful pens to encourage thoughtful comments to coworkers. The notes could be left in a mailbox, placed on a vehicle, or taped to the door of a room or office. The display can be accessible by everyone and serve as a constant reminder that kind words matter!

Promptly responding to emails, even with a simple acknowledgment of receipt, is another way to show kindness to others. It will take a minute or two out of your day, but the message you send to others is that their time is worth yours, even if you don't have the answer they need at that very moment.

Jet Stream of Kindness

"If tiny raindrops can create a flood, people can create a jet stream of kindness." These words, spoken by an eight-year-old boy affectionately named Jet Stream Jax, captured my heart. His guidance counselor, Barbara Gruener (@BarbaraGruener), tagged me in a Twitter post in the fall of 2017 with a link to his YouTube video, knowing my passion for kindness.

In the video, Jax starts out sharing his love for weather reporting, and then his words take a somber turn as he showcases the damage to his neighborhood from Hurricane Harvey and the challenges faced by his neighbors and friends at Zue S. Bales Intermediate School in Friendswood, Texas. But Jax knows that kindness can make amazing things happen. He shares a plea for others to join his Kind Coins campaign with Kids for Peace to rebuild playgrounds—not only in his community, but in others as well. His story ends with positivity, reminding the world that rainbows come after the rain.

I couldn't stop thinking about Jax's video and the courage it took for him to share his story. I showed this video to fourth- and fifth-grade students at Mechanicsville Elementary School, and they immediately wanted to help. We set up a Kind Coins collection jar, and within weeks we had filled the container. We sent in our donation, and our lives returned to the regular rhythm of work, play, and after-school activities.

For Jax and his classmates, the status quo was no longer a luxury. Because of severe flooding, several students had lost their homes. At their school, they had no playground to enjoy at recess and teachers had to provide alternative activities.

Barbara used her blog, *The Corner on Character*, to update the world with progress reports of their renovations and to share the generosity of others in their time of need. In addition to rebuilding their playground, they created a peace garden filled with colorful rocks painted and personalized by school families. They also included rocks painted to represent each school that contributed to the Kind Coins campaign for their campus.[4]

Later in the year, our students connected with Barbara and Jax via Facetime, as he took us on a tour of their new Peaceful Hearts Playground. We could hear the excitement of his words and see the joy on his face as he thanked us for our help in rebuilding his school's playground. He even showed us how to run through the new obstacle course, complete with a built-in timer! It was an incredible way to make learning relevant with kindness, while showing our students the power of words and actions.

To view Jet Stream Jax's Kind Coins video,
visit youtu.be/Pwcw3y5pKKw.

Kindness Rocks

Inspired by Jet Stream Jax and his school's Peace Garden, our students suggested that we could paint kind rocks too. Several students had discovered painted rocks throughout our community marked with an #RVArocks hashtag, representing Richmond, Virginia, and surrounding areas. This community engagement project, sparked by Henrico County Police personnel, quickly spread to an online community on Facebook where people would post the #RVArocks they found or made with clues to where they would be hidden next.[5] Our students wanted to know, "Could we paint rocks, too, and hide them around school?" Absolutely!

Several teachers in my building were interested in doing a kindness rocks lesson with their students, so we created a forty-minute lesson with two station options. One station would be a painting station, where students could create a kindness rock using rocks, paint, and paint pens. The other station would be a kind words station where students could take a cardboard heart and write a message to faculty members to be placed in their mailboxes throughout the year.

Jennifer Madison's fifth-grade class chose to do their lesson on Valentine's Day, which also corresponded with the global Random Acts of Kindness week. Our local news station, WTVR Channel 6, also arrived to showcase the lesson on its *Building Better Minds* program.[6] The morning overflowed with kindness, smiles, and joy!

Just a few hours later, tragedy struck. As our students boarded their buses to head home, their backpacks filled with valentines, another school in Florida was under lockdown with an active shooter inside.

Tragedy and Turmoil

On Wednesday, February 14, 2018, seventeen people lost their lives at Marjory Stoneman Douglas High School in Parkland, Florida, as a former student entered the campus with a fully loaded rifle. It was like living through the Sandy Hook shooting all over again. Although it wasn't my school, and wasn't even in my state of residence, I experienced the same paralyzing horror I'd felt years before.

The next day was a challenge to stay focused on our daily tasks. Educators are family. We grieve with another school's loss. We couldn't imagine the possibility of this happening to our students too.

Over the weekend, I thought about the kindness rocks we had painted with kind words on Valentine's Day. When we returned to school on Monday, Jennifer and I asked those fifth graders a question: "Could we send our kindness rocks to another school instead?" We explained, without too many details, that there was a tragedy at another school and its teachers and students might appreciate a surprise to put a smile on their faces in the midst of the turmoil. Our students readily agreed, asking if we could paint more rocks to keep *and* send.

That's what we did. We painted more rocks and chose deliberate words to help the healing process: love, joy, hope, inspire, brave. Setting aside seventeen rocks, I transformed them into memorial rocks, writing the name of each person who died that day. I made a short video of each rock, front and back, and shared

it on Flipgrid, adding the hashtag #Kind4MSD to each rock so if someone discovered a rock, they could look on Twitter to see which rock they found.

We mailed our rocks with cards, letters, and a "Be Kind" sign painted by community friends Gini Bonnell and Debbie McDonald directly to Marjory Stoneman Douglas High School. While our kind words couldn't change the events that happened that day, they showed our students that intention turned to action can lead to hope and healing.

Photo Credit: Lisa Zader
CapturedbytheLens.com

Be the Change

We often tell our students, "Be the change you want to see in the world," but what does that actually mean? For elementary students who still grapple with concrete versus abstract concepts, this phrase can be a bit of an enigma.

To "be the change," we have to live our lives with purpose, promoting kindness and joy without fear, apology, or delay. When we least expect it, one kind word or action might cause another, creating a ripple effect of kindness across our world.

After I shared our video of the kindness rocks we sent to Parkland, Florida, on Twitter, my school district saw the tweet and created its own video showcasing the memorial rocks. Another local news station, WRIC Channel 8, saw the video and asked to visit our school to talk about the activity. The next week, our students were being interviewed about kindness for a spot on the evening news.[7]

When you share your kindness story, the point is not to go viral or see how much attention you can attract. It is to find simple ways to add value to someone else's life and do it again and again and again. It's seeking the small moments and making the most of them because your small moment might be a huge moment for another person.

RAKs are about being deliberate. Being mindful. Being someone who makes a difference.

It's being the best version of you every chance you get.

Kindness Cultivator Spotlight

Barbara Gruener

Kindness Superheroes

Twitter: @BarbaraGruener

Website: corneroncharacter.blogspot.com

Inspired by the words of Gandhi to "find yourself in the service of others," Barbara Gruener, retired school counselor and character coach from Friendswood Independent School District in Friendswood, Texas, lives those words to their fullest potential. For almost two decades, she has led kindness initiatives at Bales Intermediate School and throughout her local community. Drawn to the concept of being a "bucket filler" from Carol McCloud's book, *Have You Filled a Bucket Today?,* Barbara always looks for ways to share kindness with others.

One kindness initiative that is near to her heart is her school's Knitting Club, a student group that knits caps for premature babies in developing countries. Going beyond the general expectation to be nice, these students participate in service-learning by taking action to make others' lives better.

In September 2017, Barbara's community was directly impacted by Hurricane Harvey, sparking an outpouring of love and support from others. "During an eight-month span, we had received support from caregivers, many of whom are strangers, in twenty-eight states, three countries, and a territory which, incidentally, was also recovering from hurricane devastation," she says. Each student in her school, more than five hundred students in all, received at least one card or letter expressing kind thoughts and care. "It definitely taught us how to humbly and gratefully be on the receiving end of such incredibly loving kindness."

Barbara's dedication to kindness was so great that she wrote a book about her experiences, *What's Under Your Cape? SUPERHEROES of the Character Kind*, reminding us we all can soar to great heights and become Kindness Superheroes.

To learn more about Barbara Gruener's passion
for kindness, favorite kindness quotes, and more,
visit tamaraletter.com.

Points to Ponder

 How has your community rallied together with kindness following a tragedy? What specific actions were taken to help community members heal?

Have you ever shared something online that inspired someone else? What did you share? How did you know that it was inspiring?

Who are three people you can reach out to tomorrow just to show that you care?

Chapter 4

Share Your Story

Courage is to tell the
story of who you are
with your whole heart.

—Brené Brown

I am the reason my parents got married. My mom was a freshman in college; my dad was a senior in high school. Back then it was "the right thing to do"—to get married if you found yourself in this predicament—but it was a disaster before they even began. A few months later they separated, eventually getting a divorce. My mom was single, eighteen years old, and filled with high hopes when I came into this world.

She eventually met and married another man twenty years older than she, who provided financial stability and seemed like a dream come true. Unfortunately, the age gap and insecurities caused turmoil that was seen only behind closed doors.

Countless times as a child, I was reminded that children should be seen and not heard. As the battles between my mom and stepfather escalated, I was often shushed with a glare and verbal warning to "be quiet or else," despite the rising voices and sounds of thrown items breaking in the other room. I heard words I wasn't allowed to repeat and saw alcohol-induced rage and its results. Conditioned to endure chaos and look away when situations were beyond my control, I didn't tell anyone what was happening at home until it was almost too late. Even after I gathered the courage to call the police in desperation when a violent argument went too far, the restraining order and subsequent divorce did little to provide any peace of mind. My final escape was moving to college; my mom's was an unsuccessful suicide attempt.

When you have a voice but aren't allowed to use it, you are powerless. You are ashamed. You quickly learn that your opinions don't matter, and your thoughts aren't valued by others.

For much of my life, I have struggled to abide by social etiquette regarding when and where to speak. I am a naturally boisterous person with a booming laugh, a character trait I gained from both my mom and dad. In school I would often get in trouble for talking to the person beside me; in fact, several of my report cards would begin: "Tammy is a friendly child, but she needs to be aware of disrupting others around her."

If only my teachers had known that school was my safe place to speak.

Sunday was the designated day to spend time with my dad. Because he still lived at home with his mother, I became accustomed to spending the day with her as well. Grandma Payne's house was a constant flow of friends and family members stopping by. She never shushed me or criticized my thoughts. She listened in earnest as she stood by the stove, stirring homemade gravy or making a batch of fried apples in the pan. She encouraged me to keep talking about whatever I wanted to say.

At Grandma's house, there were no rules for conversations. When she hosted her annual Christmas party, a tradition my dad and his girlfriend, Cindy, continue to this day, everyone talked at the same time over everyone else; the concept of interruption was simply a necessity for your story to be heard. When one story ended, another person jumped in to continue the tale, often relating the experience to something that happened to them. There were times when embellishment was prized more than accuracy.

On those Sundays, I found my voice. My words had meaning and value. I became a storyteller.

Like many little girls growing up, I had a diary and spent many evenings in my bedroom writing with colored pens, expressing the rush of emotions that tormented my teenage heart. It was a secure place where I could let down my guard and be the real me. I didn't have to abide by someone else's rules; I could express myself with any words I chose, without judgment, without condemnation, without consequence.

Photo Credit: Lisa Zader
CapturedbytheLens.com

I didn't worry about grammar rules or fret about passive or active voice. I simply allowed my stories to pour onto the page with fat, rounded script sometimes smeared by the tears that fell. When one journal was complete, I would purchase another. Some entries were filled with angst, others with jubilation. Writing became my refuge, my voice authentic and true.

Despite the joys of writing, it took decades before I was brave enough to share my stories with others. Free writing in a journal is different from writing for the world's consumption. In college I published a few poems in our school's literary magazine, but typing on a typewriter with no working backspace key took too long to capture my stories. If it wasn't perfect on the page, I would have to start again. I went back to journal writing, saving the formal compositions for assignments and research papers.

At that time, there was no internet, no social media. It was a different world.

Twenty years later, I was still writing, but on a portable laptop connected wirelessly to a printer. The errors were easier to fix, the global audience a click away. Each time I published a story on my blog, the temptation to chase perfection and fears of failure would resurface. I would immediately reread it, panicking when I discovered a typo or a sentence that had made sense in my head but seemed ridiculous in print.

I would edit and publish again, often repeating that process multiple times. The more I read my own writing, the more critical I became.

At times I was my own worst enemy.

Dave Burgess' insights on perfectionism, found in *Teach Like a Pirate*, echoed in my mind:

"Perfectionism can paralyze. Some people don't want to act until the time is perfect and all the bugs have been worked out. Demanding perfection keeps these people from producing anything of significance because, obviously, perfection is an impossible goal. It is far more important to be prolific than it is to be perfect."[1]

If I, as an educator, struggle with this need for perfect work to share, what message am I sending to the students I teach? Do they see me as a risk-taker or one who hides away until all conditions are perfect? Do they feel empowered to take their own risks in my classroom, to share their stories, to be authentic and vulnerable, and to open themselves up to critique?

It's a skill we need to cultivate in our students, in our co-workers, and in ourselves. Just as parents encourage their toddlers to get back up after falling over for the hundredth time, we need to encourage one another to keep putting ourselves out there, to keep pursuing our passions, and to keep telling the stories others need to hear.

Teachers Write

At some point, I realized I would be more empowered to share my stories if I could find a group of like-minded people. I joined a summer writing group led by authors Kate Messner (@KateMessner), Gae Polisner (@gaepol), and teacher-writer Jen Vincent (@mentortexts), who guided educators to step outside their comfort zones and explore writing techniques to make them better writers themselves. Each day for four weeks, we received prompts or challenges and were encouraged to share our writing with others. On Friday sessions, Polisner and others would provide feedback to those who had been willing to share their work.

Talk about being brave! It took me half the summer before I could share my writing. These were published authors reading my words and responding with such kindness! To this day the

#TeachersWrite community will always have a special place in my heart for its support during my writing journey.

Compelled Tribe

After my first summer of #TeachersWrite, Greg Armamentos (@dashthebook) continued to encourage my writing, even sending me a copy of his book, *Dash: The Life Between the Numbers.* Inspired by his kindness in running marathons honoring a blind boy named Orion, I continued to share stories with him throughout the year.

Armamentos invited me to join the Compelled Tribe writing group, led by Jennifer Hogan (@Jennifer_Hogan) and Craig Vroom (@Vroom6). Each month we were challenged to write a blog post and share on Twitter using the hashtag #CompelledTribe, tagging other members in the group. The following weeks we were asked to read and respond to other posts from writers in the group.

Being part of a writing community helped me to overcome my panic and fear of sharing my stories with the world. I still make mistakes and blush with embarrassment when I discover them, but I don't allow my fear to keep my words hidden away anymore. When someone comments on any errors in my post, I thank them for helping me become a better writer, fix the mistake, and move on.

My voice has impact and yours does too. Be brave. Share your stories.

EduMatch

About the same time that I was branching off with my writing, I was connecting with other educators on Twitter and growing my personal learning network (PLN). In discovering the digital platform Voxer, I was able to share in two-way voice communication with educators from around the world.

I joined Voxer to share an extended conversation with Sarah Thomas (@sarahdateechur), an inspiring educator with a heart for connecting others. Later that year, she created EduMatch®, a unique digital community committed to sharing and supporting one another. It was through her group that I gained more confidence in sharing my thoughts, via Voxer and by tagging EduMatch members in my posts. It was a small but effective way to find my voice and support others as they shared their stories.

For more information on EduMatch,
visit edumatch.org.

100th RAK

After completing 40 RAKs for my fortieth birthday and twenty-six RAKs for Sandy Hook, I kept the momentum going by implementing more RAKs and sharing the stories behind them. As I approached my one-hundredth random act of kindness, I wanted to make the milestone moment extra special and meaningful. I decided to take flowers to my Grandma Payne.

It was a beautiful day for a drive, and I rolled down the window to enjoy the breeze blowing through my hair. When I arrived, the birds sang their songs of spring as I gathered my flowers. It was a short walk from my car to my grandma's final resting place in the small church cemetery where several of our family members are buried. I stood for a moment in front of her granite headstone reflecting the bright sunlight, and thought about all the love she had shown me through the years. I split the bouquet of flowers in two, one for my grandma, the other for Shelby Ann.

Shelby Ann was a three-year-old girl who died in a house fire years ago. My grandma and I heard about the tragedy on the news, and we were surprised to discover she had been laid to rest right beside our family plots. We adopted her into our cemetery visits, making sure to bring her flowers too.

Although my grandma passed away almost two decades ago, I still place flowers on their graves, sweep the dirt and residue off the headstones, and pick up any stray twigs or leaves lying nearby. I take a moment to say a quick prayer of thanks, knowing each life had a purpose, no matter how long or short.

I had never seen anyone visiting Shelby Ann's grave, and the flowers and trinkets we occasionally left always seemed to go undisturbed between visits. As I grew older and became a mom myself, I couldn't fathom the unbearable pain of losing a child at such a young age. Taking flowers to a gravesite seemed the least I could do.

After completing that one-hundredth RAK, I told the story of my grandma and Shelby Ann and shared it with the world. Never in a million years did I expect to receive this response in return:

> "I just came across your blog post by chance and would like to tell you that that grave belongs to my sister. I was about a year-and-a-half when that fire broke out in my parent's trailer and took her. I have never been to her grave myself, and my mother finds it too painful. I was very moved while reading this that someone—a stranger—would put flowers on a grave of someone they didn't know. I just want to say thank you. I am just beyond words right now but thank you. —Dana"[2]

In that moment, I caught a glimpse of the power of my kindness story. Dana's sister's life mattered so much that complete strangers tended to her gravesite for almost thirty years, with no fanfare and no accolades, just to be kind. If I hadn't shared my story with the world, Dana never would have known how much her loved one meant to us. To this day, I still don't know how Dana came across my blog. I have never met her nor her family, but for that one moment of serendipity, the stars aligned perfectly for kindness to be shown to those who needed it most.

Guest Bloggers

Realizing the power of storytelling, I started a kindness blogging club at my elementary school. We were already delving into digital writing using Kidblog (which at the time was a free platform), so I knew students would be familiar with the website and how to write and publish stories. Although the school year was winding down, it would be a perfect time for students to dip their feet into the global sharing tidepool.

I asked fourth-grade and fifth-grade teachers to recommend students who might benefit from being a part of this group, and soon we were meeting to start our kindness blogging journey. On our first day, I handed out two-pocket folders labeled "Random Acts of Kindness Guest Blogger" and described our mission: to learn and grow as writers as we shared stories of kindness with the world. Our discussion began with a simple, powerful question: *"What is kindness?"*

Some students described it as a feeling:

"It's when someone does something nice for you and it makes you feel happy."

Others described the actions themselves:

"Kindness is showing you care without expecting anything else in return."

More thoughts were shared when one student crossed the threshold from saccharine to serious.

"Kindness means making sure nobody feels alone. Kindness keeps people alive."

That last phrase has haunted me ever since and fueled my commitment to kindness. To be kind, you must show a love for humanity, a compassion that surpasses any boundary of race, gender, nationality, or predisposition. Kindness reminds others of their value, their importance to this world. Kindness has the power to uplift, refill, encourage, and renew. It can indeed keep people alive.

The stories of our acts of kindness are just as powerful. The challenge is finding the courage to openly share about such experiences in a world where kindness is the exception, not the norm.

I gathered my students near as I lifted up a box that had been sitting on the adjacent table.

"Anyone want to guess what's inside my box?" I gave it a little shake, the items rattling inside, and the responses were rapid-fire.

"Toys!"

"Books!"

"Computer stuff!"

With each guess, I shook my head, my smile widening at the anticipation. Their eyes were bright and eager; they couldn't wait for me to lift the lid and reveal the hidden treasures.

At the count of three, I opened the box and pulled out each item: a small pot of packed soil, an envelope of tomato seeds, a pair of gardening gloves, a garden fork, a calendar, and a pencil.

"Today," I whispered with a twinkle in my eye, "you become Kindness Cultivators."

Making Connections

I put on the gardening gloves with a brief disclaimer: "Sometimes being a Kindness Cultivator is messy."

My wink garnered a few giggles from the students as I held the pot of dry, packed soil and turned it upside down, not a speck of dirt falling out.

"This soil is so hard! If I were to sprinkle seeds on top, what would happen?"

The group agreed that my gardening efforts would fail miserably. I opened the packet of seeds and placed a few on top, patted them down, then flipped the pot again. The seeds fell right out.

"This pot of soil is like a lot of people out there: hardened and tough. They haven't been shown any kindness in a really long time. It's up to us to loosen that soil so we can plant seeds of kindness in them. This is what makes things grow."

I grabbed the garden fork and started scraping at the soil in the pot.

"Now it might take some time to get this soil really soft, but you keep at it. You don't stop. You *cultivate* the soil by loosening it up and making a little pocket for your kindness to settle in."

I added a few seeds and continued.

"See when you pat it down, how that crumbled soil wraps itself around your seed? This keeps it safe inside until it's time for your kindness to grow."

I tilted the pot and the students watched as the planted seeds remained hidden below the soil.

"But Mrs. Letter! Why do you have a calendar in the box?"

"The calendar is a reminder that all good things take time. I can't plant seeds today and expect a garden tomorrow. I have to make sure I keep watering the soil and shining light on my seed. This will help it grow."

Satisfied with my gardening analogy, I removed my gloves and asked one final question: *"Who wants to cultivate kindness with me?"*

The Neuroscience of Kindness

Before our group composed the stories, we talked about all the different ways people show kindness to others. We discussed what it felt like when others were kind to us and how it felt when we extended that kindness to others. We even talked about times we had witnessed kindness and how that made us feel. Everyone agreed that kindness made them feel happy.

The Random Acts of Kindness Foundation showcases the "Science of Kindness" on its website. When you show, receive, or witness kindness, there are four feel-good chemicals released in your body:

Oxytocin

- Lowers blood pressure
- Improves overall heart health
- Increases self-esteem and optimism

Serotonin

- Heals wounds
- Reduces anxiety
- Maintains levels of energy

Dopamine

- Increases motivation
- Provides pleasure

Endorphins

- Reduce pain[3]

Some call the release of oxytocin, serotonin, and dopamine the "Happiness Trifecta," a natural result that occurs in your body when you experience moments of joy.[4]

Did you know there is also science behind smiling? It's true! When you smile at people, you activate their mirror neurons, an automatic response in the brain linked to a mirrored action. The recipients often start to smile without having to think about the response. They feel your smile as if they are smiling themselves, which they often do![5] Some people might choose to block the signal of communication by not returning your smile, but more often than not the smile is an automatic response.

Neuroscientist Marco Iacoboni expands on this connection of science and humanity:

"Mirroring is relevant to our tendency to be empathetic. When I see you smiling, my mirror neurons for smiling fire up, and I get your state of mind right away. I feel it as you feel it. We need that mirroring in order to create a full empathic response to other people."[6]

The field of social neuroscience is gaining more traction, and it is exciting to discover the many ways our bodies are hardwired for kindness! Think about the people you interact with each day. Do they tend to promote positivity and thoughtfulness? Or are their responses mired down with pessimism and disdain? Who we choose to spend the majority of our time with can have a direct impact on our automatic response system as mirror neurons fire up our brains to reflect what we see in others.

Be Brave

As I shared these scientific insights with my student bloggers, they nodded in agreement. Kindness made them feel great! But the challenge remained: How do we encourage others to show kindness?

We have to be brave.

Kindness cultivators step out of their comfort zones. They take a chance to make the world a better place. They know that words and actions matter. They realize that having an authentic audience transforms their message from static to dynamic. These students in my blogging group were no different than you or me. They simply needed encouragement to take those first steps.

We created screen names for our Kidblog account and discussed the differences between personal and private information: what was appropriate to share with others and what was not. It was a natural entry point for reminders of digital citizenship, a characteristic that is now a vital part of our daily communication.

Jennifer Casa-Todd emphasizes the importance of providing opportunities for students to use digital and social platforms as an integrated part of instruction in *Social LEADia: Moving Students from Digital Citizenship to Digital Leadership*:

"School should be where students not only learn about social issues, but where they are empowered to take action to make the world a better place. School should be where we help them see that they, too, can make a difference."[7]

This was the spirit I was hoping to inspire in our students, to have them see the impact of their words, their actions, their story.

Topics to Inspire

Although it was late in the school year, I offered challenges to generate ideas for student writing:

- Write one blog post about Teacher Appreciation Week (first full week in May). This could be something nice you did for your teacher or something you saw someone else do for a teacher.
- Write one blog post about Mother's Day (second Sunday in May). Tell us what thoughtful thing you did for your mom or grandmother. Don't forget to include why they are special to you!

- Celebrate others! Write a positive note to a friend or give someone a compliment, then blog about what you did.
- Memorial Day (last Monday in May). Write about an act of kindness you've done for someone in the military.
- Honor your community's citizens. Write a blog post about something nice you or someone else did for a senior citizen.

The students were excited to share their stories, even asking to skip recess to write. The activity sparked conversations about persuasive writing, stronger vocabulary choice, purpose, and passion. We all agreed that although we got a late start on the blogging, it was never too late to inspire others with stories of kindness.

Connecting with the World

As summer came and went, I continued my own kindness blogging journey, often searching online for new ideas. During one Google search, I came across a news article about an anonymous Good Samaritan who was blanketing—quite literally—the city of Boston. An image of blankets in transparent bags resting on park benches caught my eye, and I clicked on the image to read the note attached to the blankets: "These blankets are not lost! If you are cold, without shelter, and looking for comfort, then they are for you! Please take one. Enjoy and know that you are important."[8]

Intrigued, I read the article and discovered that the person behind the kind acts was a woman named Cathy O'Grady. She had intended for the kind acts to be done in anonymity, but once the news came out that it was her doing, she verified the information, stating, "If I can motivate other people to help out, that's the purpose of all this."

Each blanket included five dollars, with dozens of blankets being left for the homeless. I felt a sudden urge to connect with this woman, even though she was a complete stranger. I felt that whisper on my heart that I needed her in my world, and I was right. She is so inspirational with her words and actions!

Connecting with O'Grady and learning more about her kindness initiatives has helped me support her kindness journey, even though we have yet to meet in person. Her stories of kind acts fuel my passion as well. As my friend, Jeff Kubiak (@jeffreykubiak), likes to say, "It's Kindness Unleashed!"

Kindness Cultivator Spotlight

Cathy O'Grady

Sofia's Angels
Website: sofiasangelsfoundation.org
Facebook Group: facebook.com/sofiasangelsraok

Viewing the world from the eyes of a child can often transform our vision and purpose. When Cathy O'Grady's six-year-old son noticed a man on the streets of Boston wearing a garbage bag for a coat, his request to go home and get coats from their attic to give to the man planted a seed of kindness that would grow into a non-profit foundation dedicated to kindness.

Sofia's Angels Foundation, named for Cathy's mom, Sofia, who passed away from breast cancer, represents attributes of her mom:

"She was a gentle soul that gave with no strings attached. She loved everyone unconditionally and passed no judgment on a single person. She would go without to make sure others didn't. She was my hero, and I was lucky to call her mom."

Since its inception as a small group of friends dedicated to making the world a better place, Sofia's Angels has grown to include a global network of kindness cultivators that join together to perform acts of kindness, big and small. Using profits from two yearly fundraisers and donations from others, O'Grady and her team at Sofia's Angels have been able to change lives with their compassionate ventures, which include paying off all layaway items at a local Toys "R" Us toy store and raising $50,000 to purchase a handicapped-accessible van for a family with a medically fragile child. They enjoy scattering kindness in their community by leaving new toys at playgrounds, filling candy machines with quarters, and sharing their stories through social media to spark kind acts in others.

O'Grady often shares her passion for kindness on Facebook, where her words and insights are a continual source of inspiration. "Contrary to popular belief, kind people are not weak people. It takes strength and an awareness of personal power to be kind to people. Being kind comes from the ability to see the good in each other and to be comfortable with oneself. A person who has healthy self-esteem and a strong sense of self-worth does not need to demean others to feel good about themselves. Treating everyone with kindness take special inner fortitude and grace."

To learn more about O'Grady's passion for
kindness, favorite kindness quotes, and more,
visit tamaraletter.com.

Points to Ponder

 How do you share your stories with others? Are your stories centered around work, home, or your passions?

 Do you share your stories through digital or social media? Who are you connected with that can benefit from your stories?

Think of an act of kindness that has inspired you. What made it so impactful?

Chapter 5

Secret Sisters

We rise by lifting others.

—Robert Ingersoll

In the realm of social media, news about our students and families travels faster than ever before. Often our first point of contact about something that happens in our community isn't in our email inbox or the evening news; it's a screenshot or text message sent with lightning speed.

Such was the case of the passing of a student in our community. Nate Metheny, a bright-eyed, joyful six-year-old unexpectedly suffered a medical crisis from which he couldn't recover. Diagnosed with Williams Syndrome years before, his heart simply stopped beating. His mom, Diane, posted a plea for prayer on Facebook as he was being airlifted to the hospital, which was followed by another post shortly thereafter that Nate had passed away.

To learn more about Williams Syndrome,
visit williams-syndrome.org.

As school leaders, we have crisis plans in place with how-to guides on next steps for helping our school community begin the healing process after loss. But what support parameters are in place for the families of those who suffer the most?

A Year of Blessings

I found myself in a quandary, paralyzed by the desire to help but unsure of what to do. Dinners were made and cards were written, but it didn't seem enough. I felt immobile and powerless in my feeble attempts to offer comfort and care, knowing the family's journey of grief had only just begun.

I was sharing my angst with another friend of mine, Michele Henry, who was also feeling the weight at a loss as to what to do next. We knew we wanted to offer support and kindness to the family, but how? Sometimes the brightest spark of inspiration shines when you find yourself in the deepest depth of darkness.

With a bit of brainstorming, we crafted a plan of action. We selected ten women who knew the family, either as neighbors, coworkers, or friends, and asked if they would like to join our undercover mission of kindness. It was in that moment that Secret Sisters came to life.

The plan was actually quite simple. Each of us would choose one month on the calendar to shower the family with kindness in three ways:

1. Pray for the family daily;
2. Show a small act of kindness once a week like sending a card or writing a note, leaving it in a location to be discovered by family members;
3. Carry out one additional act of kindness in Nate's memory or provide for a family experience.

We signed all cards and correspondence: "Secret Sisters", a group of individuals working together as one. Many of us started this journey as strangers, but by the end we were family.

Our acts of kindness ranged from simple to complex. We mailed packages and left surprises on their doorstep. (When was the last time you went to someone's house at midnight to ding-dong-ditch? Let me tell you, it's a bit more nerve-wracking when you are in your forties!)

We donated books to the school library and made donations to the Williams Syndrome Foundation, all in Nate's name. Restaurant gift cards. Ladybug wind chimes. Gifts for laughter, gifts for love. It was a year of healing for Nate's family; it was a year of healing for us.

Connecting Online

To stay connected, Michele and I created a Facebook group and invited only the Secret Sisters to join. Each person selected a preferred month to bless the family, and each month the designated Secret Sister would post what she did, often with photos to document the kindness, and we would follow up by brainstorming more ideas.

Some members posted links about grief recovery to help us grow our empathy and guide us as we struggled with what to say and not to say. Other members posted inspiring quotes and uplifting messages, shining a light of positivity through the journey. We shared our sorrow over not being able to do enough; we shared our joy in reassurance that small acts were better than none. We made note of milestone moments that might be more painful than others. First holidays as a family of four instead of five were especially difficult to endure.

Then came the day when Nate's mom, Diane, posted a note on her Facebook page, thanking the Secret Sisters for their kindness. Since I was connected to Diane on Facebook (we used to sing in chorus together years ago), I took a screenshot of her post and shared it on our Secret Sisters page.

Diane Workman Metheny
18 minutes ago

Whoever you are, 'Secret Sisters', know that you have blessed our family - Thank you!

We were elated to see a glimmer of light shared by Diane! Her posts of gratitude filled us up as we continued to shower her family with kindness. We hoped they knew they were not alone in their grief.

Revealing Identities

As the one-year anniversary of Nate's passing approached, we wanted to do something extraordinary, to give the family something to look forward to after their day of remembrance. We decided it was time to reveal our identities in person.

We planned a potluck celebration at a local park. To remain anonymous until the big reveal, we created a Secret Sisters Gmail account for the family to correspond with us. We crafted an invitation using a blank puzzle, which we then broke apart into pieces and mailed to the family, in hopes that they would work together to solve the puzzle and discover our final gift.

When the reveal date arrived, the Secret Sisters gathered at the park, many of us meeting in person for the first time. Some members of our group couldn't attend, but we felt their presence just the same. We covered the picnic tables with our side dishes and desserts and awaited the arrival of Diane, her husband Kevin, and their daughters, Kaitlyn and Caroline.

Our tears of sorrow transformed into tears of joy. There were gasps of surprise as Diane and Kevin finally saw who was behind the mask of Secret Sisters. The reveal was overwhelming; they had no idea there were twelve individuals working together as one.

As we sat down to share a meal together, we had an opportunity to share stories of how our year unfolded, from minor mishaps to confessions of secrecy now open for all to see. It was a time of closure and new beginnings; compassion and empathy merged together as strength and support. There were tears once again, but of overwhelming gratitude for the bond that was created through a year of giving.

Sharing Our Story

I was very hesitant to write about Secret Sisters. I didn't want anyone to think we were trying to take credit for the whispers God had placed on our hearts. Our initial feelings of empathy were replaced by the nudge of compassion; we simply followed through by making it happen.

But what if there was someone else out there who needed the love and kindness of a community to help them through the heartache and despair of loss? What if our story could plant a seed of kindness in someone else to do something similar? Was it possible to share our story without the spotlight being on us as people, but the purpose instead?

With permission from the Metheny family and others in the group, I wrote a blog post about our experience as Secret Sisters.[1] I shared it on Facebook and prayed there wouldn't be any negative comments. Much to my relief, the response was overwhelmingly positive. Several people who followed Diane on Facebook had seen her Secret Sisters posts throughout the year and were delighted to discover the many hands who lifted her family in their greatest time of need.

As I continued to share our story with others, it created a ripple effect of kindness through our community to others nationwide. It was humbling to see Nate's legacy live on as other people took this concept and made it their own. I received emails and text messages from friends and strangers, sharing the various ways they were blessing their neighbors and coworkers as a unified, secret group. They, too, were embracing the we-before-me concept. Even Nate's older sister, Kaitlyn, formed a Secret Sisters group of her own to bless a local family the following year. The ripple effect was endless.

Through the support of the Random Acts of Kindness Foundation, Secret Sisters was featured on public radio as Erica Lantz shared our experiences on Boston's WBUR Kind World program.[2] Remembering Nate and the ways we wrapped this family with love reminded me yet again how important it is for us to transform intention into action.

To listen to Diane and Kevin Metheny's story on Kind World, visit wbur.fm/2km3oEv.

Tragedies happen every day. With the advent of social media and technological advances, we have instant access to news, good and bad. What are we doing to make the world a better place when tragedies occur? What's our response? Do we pause for a moment to think about the ramifications to others, or do we scroll to the next headline and push it out of our minds?

Boomerang Effect

Two years after Nate passed away, my mom was diagnosed with stage four lung cancer. Months later, my mother-in-law entered hospice, her battle with colon cancer coming to an end. It was an overwhelming time in my world, with illness and death closing in on every front.

As an adult, I have always been open about sharing the joys and struggles in my life with others, but this was different. My husband and I were losing our moms at the same time, while also having to maintain a stable environment for our three children as we worked full-time jobs. The pain was excruciating at times as we struggled to be everything for everyone when they needed us the most.

As Rich's mom became bedridden and my mom struggled to breathe, the sense of urgency for making memories was overwhelming. I tried to capture even the smallest of moments, with photos on Facebook and Instagram or sharing stories on my blog, so that I could be reminded later that dying wasn't only about death but about living as well.

In one post, I shared photos of my mom visiting my Tiny Tech Cafe, her smile radiant as she sat in a wheelchair. It was the first, and only, time she had visited my classroom. After a quick tour of the room, we left, making our way towards the hallway ramp. I can still remember my mom's laughter as we stood at the top of the ramp, her voice urging me to "let go so I can fly." I did as she asked and down the ramp she rolled, her squeals of delight forever captured in my heart.

One of the Secret Sisters, Laurie Sanderson, messaged me saying she wanted to create a memory for me and my mom. "I want to bless you with Sunday tea at the Jefferson." It was an overwhelming gesture of kindness that I almost turned down, my pride nearly preventing me from being blessed by my friend.

The Jefferson Hotel, a historic landmark in Richmond, Virginia, was one of my mom's favorite places to dine. Elegant and detailed, a meal at The Jefferson represented fine dining at its best. The first time she and I shared a meal there was when I turned eighteen years old. The second time was when I surprised her with a meal for her sixtieth birthday. Despite our mutual love for the iconic hotel, we had only been there twice together.

At the time Laurie contacted me, my mom was struggling with her physical demise. Waiting to learn if her cancer had returned, and if additional treatments would be possible, weighed heavily on our hearts and minds. Each day was harder to walk, harder to stand, harder to talk, harder to breathe. It was excruciating being a bystander to her decline.

Laurie's act of kindness was incredible. Not only did she arrange for a Sunday tea experience for me and my mom during a season when reservations are hard to come by, but she also covered the cost and tip.

"Just go, enjoy yourself, and make memories," she told me. "That's what matters most."

When we arrived at The Jefferson Hotel that beautiful fall day, her smile beamed so brightly that complete strangers commented on her joy. This, of course, made her smile even more! With her decreased stability, we both agreed it was best to stay in the wheelchair for the tea, an accommodation already anticipated by hotel staff.

After being led to our seating area, our waiter presented my mom with a surprise.

"This was sent for the woman with the beautiful smile," he said.

In his hands was a small wrist corsage with two perfectly shaped roses. Oh, if you could have seen my mom in that moment! You would have thought she had been crowned homecoming queen! I discovered later that Laurie had included the corsage as a gift for my mom—a small, but perfect, addition to our day.

The next two hours were filled with laughter, sweet treats, and priceless memories. Laurie's thoughtful act of kindness was so much more than an afternoon tea; her generosity gave us a reprieve from dying and death. Her kindness restored our souls.

How can we share the waves of life's turbulence with one another? It begins with connection. Whether through work or school, online platforms, in-person social events, or random check-ins with family and friends, staying connected with others is important. We need to make an investment in other people's lives because it is tough to go through this journey alone!

Kindness Cultivator Spotlight

Staci Erickson
#kindness180
Twitter: @stacitoday
Instagram: stacitoday

Sometimes the greatest gift of kindness is sparked in the most unlikely place. This was the case for Staci Erickson, a middle school math instructional coach with Perryton Independent School District in Perryton, Texas, who saw a social media post by Ron Clark in Atlanta, Georgia, that a father of one of their students desperately needed a kidney. The post was brief and to the point, a plea that resonated with Staci: "This is one of the best fathers in the world and he needs your help!"

Moved to action, Staci contacted a kidney transplant center, got tested, and discovered she was a perfect match to donate a kidney to this stranger. On September 28, 2017, she gave the gift of life to Carlos Copeland, as the kidney transplant was successfully completed. "I think too many times we overthink things. This man needed a kidney and I had two. . . . Sometimes simply looking in the eyes of a person in need and listening to their story will make those hard decisions to help all of a sudden extremely easy."

Staci also created the Kindness 180 challenge, providing 180 kindness challenges for others to complete during a traditional school year. "When someone has 'done a 180,' it means they have changed their behavior or thoughts about someone or something." She has applied the Kindness 180 challenge to her own life, learning to be kind to others in the face of adversity and embracing forgiveness instead of pain. "Kindness 180 is about showing kindness to people who inspire you, but it is also pushing yourself to show kindness even when you don't really want to."

Teachers at Staci's school were encouraged to complete at least five kindness challenges with their students each semester. They also distributed "Kindness Crew" stickers to those who went above and beyond to show kindness to others. By sharing their acts of kindness on social media using the hashtag #kindness180, their kind acts could scatter around the world to inspire others too!

To learn more about Staci Erickson's passion for kindness, favorite kindness quotes, and more, visit tamaraletter.com.

Points to Ponder

 Can you think of a time when a family from your school community suffered great loss? How did your school community respond? What support structures are in place for helping these families heal?

 Do any ideas from Secret Sisters spark a light of inspiration that you might want to implement as a plan of support for families dealing with loss?

When was a time in your life when someone showed you compassion in a time of great need?

Chapter 6

Renee's Cheerios

A little glitter can turn
your whole day around.

—Junie B. Jones

One of the joys of working with children is the realization that you have the power to impact their lives in a positive way. Your legacy as an educator is not in what you do, but whom you serve! Think about how many children cross your path each day: in the hallways, in your classroom, during assemblies and activities. Simple acts of kindness can transform a student's day: a genuine smile, a greeting by name, a high-five, or holding the door open.

Every act of kindness matters.

As an elementary teacher, you are with the same students every day for five to six hours a day. That's a lot of time to form strong relationships with students in your class. You teach them all subjects and guide them in their mastery of social expectations, classroom organization, and individual responsibilities. You help mold their basic understanding of group dynamics and social-emotional learning. You are their teacher, but also their nurse, safety officer, counselor, and more.

At the secondary level, you interact with hundreds of students a day. Many will pass your room as they walk from one class to the next; the chosen ones enter and stay. You, too, have the opportunity to develop strong relationships with your students, but your methods are vastly different from those of an elementary teacher. Your time is limited, and your students are older. They can connect and share with you in ways younger students cannot.

At all levels your knowledge surpasses surface level demographics. You learn about their pets, listen to their weekend activities, peek into their passions. You celebrate their successes and support them in their challenges.

You recognize the importance of pronouncing your students' names correctly and use their names often in conversation. You meet them at the door with a smile in the morning and provide a high-five as they leave for the day.

You discover aspects of their lives that break your heart. You listen as they share whispered stories about what happened before they caught the bus to school. You share a hug and wipe away tears when the words don't even come. You realize which students need new shoes, new coats, or new school supplies and do whatever it takes to get them these essentials.

You are their teacher, but you are so much more.

You are the one who meets their academic, social, and emotional needs 180 days of the year. For many of those students, your support continues through holidays and extended breaks.

You notice which students arrive hungry and how that impacts their learning. According to the United States Department of Agriculture, 30.4 million children daily receive reduced-price or free meals.[1] In 2017, 6.5 million children in the United States resided in food-insecure households,[2] where meals were either reduced in quality, variety, or desirability, or there was reduced food intake with disrupted eating patterns.[3] Childhood hunger is no longer an isolated dilemma; it's prevalent around the world.

We are reminded of Maslow's Hierarchy of Needs.[4] The base of the pyramid consists of physiological needs that must be met first. Once the foundation is set, psychological needs must be met before one can reach the top of the pyramid to achieve the fullest potential of self-actualization.

Maslow's Hierarchy of Needs

Self-Actualization

- Achieving one's fullest potential

Esteem Needs

- Feelings of accomplishment

Belongingness and Love Needs

- Relationships with others

Safety Needs

- Security and safety

Physiological Needs

- Food, water, shelter, rest

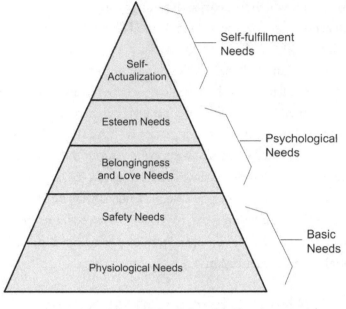

Adapted from Sam McCleod
"Maslow's Hierarchy of Need"

Maslow's Before Bloom's

In 1956, a cognitive taxonomy was created based on the research of Benjamin Bloom. Using a similar hierarchy as the image above, it placed the academic concepts and levels of learning at the foundation of the pyramid, rising up with the advanced complexities of learning and processing at the top. Fifty years later, this structure was updated to focus on action verbs instead of static nouns with a flip of the top two tiers.[5]

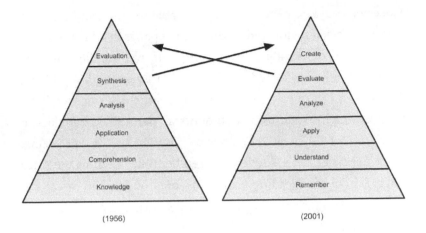

Adapted from Ricky Pradhan
"Application of Bloom's Taxonomy in E-Learning"

Which of these pyramids best represents your focus? Are you content-driven, people-driven, or a balance of both? Educators are called to do so much more than simply transfer knowledge from our brains to our students. We must meet their academic, social, and emotional needs, all while preparing them for success in an ever-changing world.

Some might say this is an impossible task, and there are days I would agree. But over the course of an entire school year, the teachers who make the greatest impact are those who understand the need to focus on Maslow's before Bloom's.

Renee's Cheerios

Renee Parr, a first-grade teacher at Mechanicsville Elementary School in Virginia, understood the importance of Maslow's before Bloom's. Each morning as she scanned her room for students without a snack, she called them to her desk to receive a small bag of

Cheerios. She knew they wouldn't be able to concentrate on her lessons if they were focused on the hunger pangs in their stomachs.

Renee's exuberant personality and welcoming smile were contagious to all who knew her. She greeted others with a jubilant, "Hi, friend!" as they passed in the hall, often raising her hand to give a high-five to former students as she walked her class to lunch. Everyone knew Renee; her passion for life was energizing. A former cheerleader, she volunteered her time coaching the Atlee High School cheerleading team and doted on her three-year-old daughter, Avery, reminding her, "No bow, no go!" Renee brought a sparkle of light to dreary days.

Renee was also passionate about kindness, gathering with friends at Christmastime to perform acts of kindness around her community. They would leave gift cards for strangers on the shelves of Target or purchase toys for families in need. They delighted in the knowledge that they were putting good into the world.

Then in July 2014, tragedy struck. While sharing a meal with her father and daughter in a local restaurant, Renee felt ill and collapsed in the parking lot as they tried to leave. She was rushed to the hospital. Despite the best efforts of medical staff, the family was told there was nothing more they could do. They would have to let her go.

As her husband, Zach, stood by her side, he felt a connection to her spirit as a conversation passed in his heart and mind with Renee. She was in the early stages of pregnancy carrying their second child, news they had yet to share with the world.

"I knew in that moment that her passing was somehow connected to the baby she was growing inside. Her voice whispered to me that we had to divide and conquer. I would stay with Avery and she would go with the baby. It spoke to the kind of person she was—always giving of herself in every way."[6]

Renee passed away at the age of thirty, her death incomprehensible. The shock waves continued as news spread, leaving a gaping hole in the heart of our community.

How does one heal from loss? We asked this question repeatedly. In an instant, this vibrant, larger-than-life personality was gone, and we struggled to pick up the pieces and move forward.

Her funeral was filled to capacity with mourners wearing her favorite color, purple, in a celebration of her life. Her mom, LaVerne, affectionately known as LaLa to many, donned a sparkling tiara and gave the eulogy, sharing favorite memories of her princess. The pain was raw and overwhelming.

Following the funeral, we were left to answer the question no one wanted to ask: Now what?

Perspectives of Grief

Grief is a stranger to no one. At some point in our lives, we will encounter heartbreaking sorrow that cuts us to the core. It might be the loss of a family member, coworker, neighbor, or friend. It might be the loss of a pet, a job, a home. Grief hits us with a gut-wrenching punch to the stomach and tosses us in turbulence as we grapple with unanswered questions. Sometimes grief leaves us unable to move forward with our daily lives.

Our perspectives change when grief takes a stronghold. We catch a glimpse of our own mortality, and our realities of yesterday become memories for today. The impact of death escapes no one; it's a journey of juxtaposition with highs and lows.

The summer before my sixth year of teaching, I was delighted to discover I was pregnant with my second child. I began the school year with a tiny baby bump, my third-grade class already suggesting baby names before we knew if it was a boy or a girl.

Then came that awful day when the regularly scheduled doctor's appointment couldn't find the heartbeat we had heard the month before. I was sent to the hospital for more in-depth analysis, only to learn the child we had hoped and prayed for remained in my womb, but silent and still.

Surgery was scheduled; the days and weeks following were a blur. I took sick leave from work to recover physically and emotionally from the unfathomable event that would mark my perspectives of grief and motherhood for the rest of my life. What pulled me through the darkest days were my faith, my family, and my community of friends at school.

Kindness was ever-present. Teachers graded my papers. Dinners arrived at my door. I received heartwarming notes from others who had also miscarried children. I was reminded that I wasn't alone in my grief.

We quickly conceived again, suffering another miscarriage weeks before Christmas. It was almost too much to bear. It was then that I received a surprise in the mail.

It was a delicate angel ornament for my Christmas tree from a woman I had interacted with in an online chat forum but had never met. She and I were due on the same date, but when I had my miscarriage, it was too painful for me to continue chatting in the group. Her empathy for my heartache was an act of kindness that resonates with me even today. Each year I display her ornament on my Christmas tree, a reminder that lost does not mean forgotten.

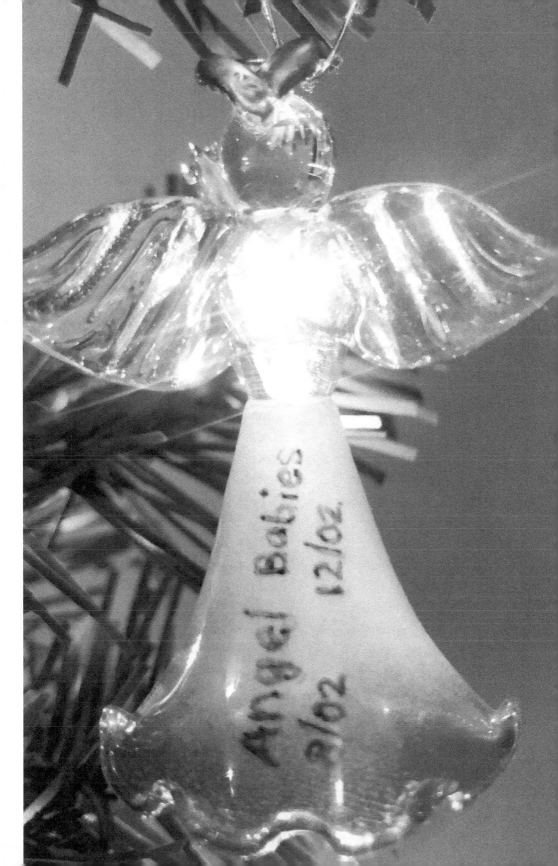

Five Stages of Grief

Many times in our lives, we are not allowed to pursue Option A. Maybe it's the broken heart of a breakup or the trials of transition. Perhaps it's the door that closes on a future opportunity. How do we overcome disappointment and grief when they appear as roadblocks on our life journey?

In *Option B: Facing Adversity, Building Resilience, and Finding Joy,* Sheryl Sandberg and Adam Grant write, "Grief doesn't share its schedule with anyone; we all grieve differently and in our own time."[7] I think that's the most difficult part of understanding loss and grief. It's challenging, but necessary, to realize that our experiences of grief might not match anyone else's timeline or meet their expectations.

Elisabeth Kübler-Ross, a Swiss-American psychiatrist, shared her research about grief in her book, *On Death and Dying: What the Dying Have to Teach Doctors, Nurses, Clergy and Their Own Families.* Commonly coined "The Five Stages of Grief," Kübler-Ross noted that in the midst of the five stages of denial, anger, bargaining, depression, and acceptance, one emotion was evident throughout:

Hope.[8]

Grief is messy, but the kindness of someone else can be that ray of hope to pull someone through the toughest of times. Because grief is sometimes unpredictable, it's difficult for others to know how to reach out or what to do. You want to help the person who is crushed under the weight of sorrow, but what about the others who are also impacted by the loss? How does one heal the heart while also rebuilding a community?

We do it together.

Stages of Grief

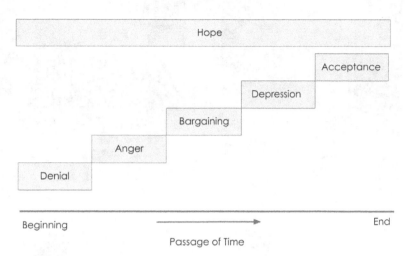

Beginning   End

Passage of Time

Renew and Restore

A month after Renee died, we returned to our buildings to set up for a new school year. The students on her roster were reassigned to another teacher, her classroom now occupied by a dear friend who changed grade levels to be in her room. One wall displayed a quote from one of Renee's favorite children's books, *Junie B., First Grader: Shipwrecked*:

"A little glitter can turn your whole day around."

As a school community, we needed time to renew and restore. Our hearts were broken, and every milestone was a memory of Renee. That year our principal, Amy Robinson, declared our only focus was "love one another and be kind." We were reminded that grief impacts us differently and encouraged to show kindness to one another as a support system.

Our grief was a shared experience that brought us closer as a school community. We let go of petty disputes and intentionally focused on the healing of the heart. When one teacher felt the unexpected woes of heartache, another teacher covered her classroom so she could have a moment to breathe again. We became mindful of the stages of grief and more empathetic to those who struggled to regain their footing.

The local community felt the loss as well. Shortly after her passing, a memorial fund was created to honor Renee and her seven years of service to her school. In lieu of flowers, everyone was asked to donate to *Renee's Cheerios* with 100 percent of profits funneling back to serve students at Mechanicsville Elementary School. Today, four years after Renee's death, students at our school continue to benefit from her legacy. The money has been used to purchase school supplies, field trip fees, eyeglasses, coats, shoes, and snacks. It's also been used to fund yearly scholarships for rising sixth graders and kindness passion projects so students can experience the joys of giving to others.

Signs of Sparkle

We discovered through our time of communal loss that signs of sparkle around our campus brought joy as we remembered Renee's life. A purple wind chime was added to a tree by the cafeteria, its lilting sound a sweet reminder of Renee's laughter. Purple glitter was sprinkled around our flagpole as we dedicated our Mechanicsville

Photo Credit: Lisa Zader, CapturedbytheLens.com

Miler Fun Run in her name. We custom-designed purple "MES Staff" shirts with a pink tiara resting on the M.

Parents and students left mementos around the huge oak tree that stretched its limbs across the entrance to the parking lot, and even now a glittered, lavender bow is wrapped around the trunk—a daily reminder that Renee's spirit still sparkles. We received a donation of two custom-made purple benches with a small tiara carved out of the metal to add to our learning garden.

Photo Credit: Lisa Zader, CapturedbytheLens.com

During the holidays, we displayed an evergreen tree in our school lobby, complete with purple ribbon and lots of sparkle. Many of the ornaments were handmade, several with Renee's monogram shining in purple glitter, a symbol representing the joy she brought to our lives each day. Our school donated children's books to her husband and daughter for their first Christmas without Renee, a reminder of her love for reading.

There is no set timeline for grief and healing. One day all seems well, and the next you find yourself inconsolable at the silliest of things. It's important to give yourself, and others around you, an extra dose of grace and patience during times of struggle. Be kind, for everyone you meet is fighting a battle you know nothing about. Even those who share the same traumatic experiences might have varied responses from day to day.

In *Be REAL: Educate from the Heart*, Tara Martin shares the pain she experienced when her father unexpectedly lost his life under tragic circumstances. In describing her journey with grief, she shares how it translates into the classroom with students:

To prepare our students with skills of empathy and connection, we must model those skills for them. We must share our experiences of overcoming challenges, because doing so helps others gain strength and encouragement.[9]

Allyson Apsey (@AllysonApsey) expands on this mindset in *The Path to Serendipity: Discover the Gifts along Life's Journey*:

Sometimes people just need someone to hear them out as they sort through a problem . . . One of the most powerful questions in the history of human relationships is made up of four simple words: How can I help?[10]

Renee's Legacy

What I have learned through these experiences of grief and despair is the power of kindness to uplift and inspire. Whether in times of tragedy or times of joy, the communal heartbeat of others pulls you through. Kindness surpasses all walls of resistance; it changes perspectives and promotes peacefulness. To be kind to others is to show that their lives matter and have value. May we all embrace Renee's spirit of kindness and friendship to many.

Kindness Cultivator Spotlight

Erin Schricker
Bunnies of Hope

It's always a joy to see the different ways students and teachers embrace kindness and extend it to others. While a focus on kindness may start in the home, the classroom, or the workplace, it's such a delight to see kindness sprinkling like confetti in this world!

Erin Schricker, a high school student in Mechanicsville, Virginia, began cultivating kindness at the age of fourteen, making felt bunnies for family and friends. When her grandmother was diagnosed with cancer, Erin crafted a pink felt bunny for breast cancer awareness and attached a name tag with one inspirational word: Courage. This was the spark for her kindness outreach, Bunnies of Hope.

Erin makes each bunny by hand, tracing the pattern on felt and sewing the pieces together with matching thread. Each bunny includes googly eyes and a Bible verse to correspond with the chosen word on the name tag. She began delivering them to patients at Martha Jefferson Hospital in Charlottesville, Virginia, but hopes to expand her project to include additional hospitals in the future.

"I frequently hand them out to people who are going through a hard time. Each time I hear a story of how a bunny has brought joy and strength to a patient, I feel all the more inspired to keep sewing. Comforting people is what Bunnies of Hope exists for, and as long as these bunnies keep inspiring and uplifting, I will keep going!"

Erin's passion for kindness inspires others as well. "Kindness is not as hard as you think! You don't have to start a charity or even do one specific thing all the time. Always know that your kindness makes more of an impact than you realize!"

To learn more about Erin Schricker's passion for kindness, favorite kindness quotes, and more, visit tamaraletter.com.

Points to Ponder

 What is the legacy you will leave behind? How do you hope others remember you?

Who has made a life-changing impact on you? Why?

How can you show Maslow's over Bloom's in your workplace, home, and community?

Section 2

Cultivating Kindness

I've learned that people will forget what you said, people will forget what you did, but people will never forget how you made them feel.

—Maya Angelou

Chapter 7

Tilling the Soil

What you do makes a
difference, and you have
to decide what kind of
difference you want to make.

—Jane Goodall

Reflecting on my younger years, I'm always amazed at the "flashbulb memories" that are frozen in time. You might have those instances as well, when the memory of a moment is captured like the flash of a light: instantaneous, precise, permanent. The phrase, first coined by psychologists Roger Brown, PhD, and James Kulik, PhD, in 1977, describes the natural phenomenon where an emotional response to an event is so vivid, the moment is captured with extraordinary details as if looking at a photograph.[1] These flashbulb memories often are in response to an intense, devastating event such as 9/11, but other times they result from something that occurs on a more personal level when physical emotions are heightened.

One of my favorite flashbulb memories involved me and my dad. In the corner of his bedroom, he kept a wide, glass, Lance canister on the floor where he would keep his spare change. As a child, I was mesmerized by this growing collection of coins and would spend hours meticulously organizing and counting, grouping coins by type or year.

One Sunday my dad asked me to pull out all the quarters and put them in a pile. The jar was almost full of coins, so it took some time to fulfill his request, but I finally sorted through the stack and had more quarters than I could hold in both hands.

"Let's get you a bag," he told me. "We're going to spend all those quarters at the arcade."

It was one of the most magical days I ever spent with my dad. He took me to all his favorite places (Including the Moose Lodge!) and we played every video game, pinball machine, and quarter poker challenge we could find. He gave me complete freedom of choice in spending the money, and he joined in the fun. Almost forty years later, I can still hear our laughter melding together.

That day I learned a few lessons about kindness from my dad:

You don't have to be wealthy to make someone feel rich.

While our quarter collection was quite impressive in the mind of an eight-year-old, it wasn't about the money, but the experience. My dad used the element of surprise and the novelty of a shared passion for gaming to create a lifelong memory for me.

Time Is a precious commodity.

My dad chose to spend his day with me. He joined in my fun and played an active role in the memory-making. He introduced me to the regulars who sat in his favorite establishments and shared that this was "our day to have fun." He made me feel like I was the most important person in the entire world. We are all so busy these days with work, school, and community commitments. Carve out time to embrace spontaneity and surprise.

You can scatter seeds of kindness everywhere.

While there are no longer arcade rooms in the back of a Peaches record store, there are still gumball machines at the grocery store and dollar stores where a child can buy anything in the store for only four quarters before tax. Imagine your child's jubilation to suddenly know they can spend a little money on whatever they want—just because! What joy! You could take it a step further and allow your child to spend money on themselves *and* commit a RAK for someone else. Each time I hide a dollar bill in the toy section of The Dollar Tree or scatter pennies for wishes near a fountain bubbling with water, I am reminded of my dad's kindness shining through me.

Another flashbulb memory was at the start of my teaching career in North Las Vegas, Nevada. My husband and I had driven across the country from Florida to Nevada in separate vehicles while our belongings were transported by the military. The air was stifling hot, a triple-digit day in the desert. As we pulled into the parking lot of our temporary home, the wheels of our car spun a cloud of dusty sand across the asphalt. Everything was brown and barren, a far cry from the lush, tropical palm trees that lined our streets just the week before.

Arriving at my new school the following week, I stared in shock at the dry, cracked land that looked like an overbaked potato and wondered how on earth anything could grow with such a dense foundation. The comparison struck me then as it does now:

A hardened foundation is only suitable for the rugged and the tough.

A nutrient-rich soil nourishes so much more.

It was the first decision I made as a first-year teacher: to create a classroom culture of kindness to nourish the needs of all my students.

Hanover Tomatoes

In my hometown of Hanover County, Virginia, we grow tomatoes. Lots and lots of tomatoes. The quality of soil matters for a substantial harvest. Our local farmers also grow other forms of produce that you can see proudly displayed at the Pole Green Produce stand, but tomatoes take center stage in the summer. The tomatoes have grown in such popularity they are referred to as "Hanover Tomatoes" and even have their own Wikipedia page, a Tomato Bowl football game, and a local festival that draws a crowd of more than forty thousand attendees. Pretty impressive for produce that grows on a vine!

What makes a Hanover Tomato different from all the rest? While the fruit itself is juicy and sweet, it's the soil that creates optimal conditions for perfection. Described by *The Washington Post* as a "sandy, Coastal Plain type of soil" east of the Fall Line, the soil in Hanover County retains less water than other soil types, which in turn lowers the pH level and produces a higher level of acid.[2] Coupled with an environment of high humidity, bright sunlight, and temperate heat, the Hanover Tomato thrives in our locality.

Much like the soil of an award-winning Hanover Tomato, we have to work a bit to create a foundation that is optimal for growth. Simply setting something on top of the soil isn't going to make it grow! Whether in a classroom, a workplace, or at home, it's important to till the soil. We need to look at the foundation we've created and ask ourselves if the soil is too firm. We might need to turn it over and break it up to make it soft again. Maybe your soil is great, but you want to add something that needs to be evenly distributed. Are you making small changes or a complete overhaul for new growth?

There are times when tilling the soil is easy, and you can do it on your own with a deep spade or a cultivator fork. Other times you need help from others with more tools and expertise. Shaping culture requires cultivating. Put on your gardening gloves. Grab your hand tool. Find a small section of soil and till. Not too rough. Not too soft. Just right. The goal is to loosen the soil—distribute, not destroy.

Shift the Rock

There are times, however, when even our best attempts at cultivating a positive climate for change reveals a rock that just won't move. The deeper we dig, the more rock is uncovered, and we are tempted to curse the rock for its rigid, oppressive hindrance to progress. We might even say we hate the rock for standing in our way. *Why can't the rock understand why it needs to move? Who put this rock here in the first place? This rock is the most annoying rock I have ever encountered in my entire life!*

Sometimes in tilling the soil of culture, we have to learn how to get along with people that misunderstand our purpose, argue with our passion, and purposefully try to block any attempts at change.

How do we respond to those rocks in our soil? Do we abandon the land and move? Do we dig deeper, hoping the rock will miraculously move on its own? In working with a variety of climates and conditions for the past two decades, this is my best advice when you encounter resistance from others while tilling the soil:

Assume positive intent.
A wise friend of mine always reminds me of this phrase whenever I get caught up in others' perceived negativity. Believe it or not, that rock in your path might have nothing to do with you! The

You can be the
sweetest
tomato on the vine,
but there will still be
people
who don't like
tomatoes.

negativity we encounter in other people could spring from challenges in their lives, completely removed from us. Just as the rock
is not intentionally trying to be a hindrance to your work, it might
be there for another purpose. It might need to be moved by someone else.

Seek to understand.

When tilling the soil, we might not have all the information we
need in the moment when we encounter resistance. Ask questions
to learn more about the "why," listening with an open heart to the
reasoning. Digging a little deeper can help uncover the root of an
issue, which helps to create a new plan for cultivation.

Be flexible.

Even the most experienced farmers know that weather can play
havoc on crops. Sometimes we have to shift our action plans for

unforeseen conditions that arise. Rather than bemoaning the fact that our plans changed, make the necessary shifts and keep moving forward.

Stay positive.

It's a challenge to look on the bright side when a rock blocks all the sunlight. The sunlight is still there, just on the other side! If you feel yourself being suffocated by the darkness, turn the other way and look at the light.

Persevere.

The path of greatest resistance often reaps the greatest rewards. If you are working towards something you feel passionate about, others will soon share that passion and pick up a spade to help. Share your struggles. Be open to suggestions for a better path. Most of all, don't give up! Right in that moment when you think the rock will never move, that's when the shift occurs.

Cultivating Kindness

What I love about these strategies for tilling the soil is that we can have ownership of them all, and they can help us overcome the negativity of others. In a nation overflowing with freedoms and rights, it's helpful to recognize those moments when we can be a catalyst for positive change, even in the most difficult of situations.

When I first started cultivating kindness as described in Chapter 2, I felt awkward sharing my stories with others. What if people reacted negatively? What if they thought I was trying to bring attention to myself instead of kindness in general? What if they criticized my writing skills and missed the whole point completely?

Those "what ifs" will eat you alive! Doubt is a powerful weapon in the destruction of our dreams. Never doubt the impact of your passion and purpose! Those seeds that are planted in you are meant to bloom and scatter to others.

One way we can do this is by remembering how to CULTIVATE kindness in others:

C–Compassion

U–Understand

L–Listen

T–Take Time

I–Inspire

V–Value

A–Accept

T–Teach

E–Empathy

C Is for Compassion

When discussing kindness, the words compassion and empathy are often used interchangeably, but they actually have different meanings. Empathy is focused more on the feelings you have for someone else when they are going through a crisis or need. Compassion takes empathy one step further and includes the desire to act to make the situation better.[3] Empathy is the why; compassion is the what.

Sometimes described as "suffering together," compassion has a biological basis, releasing chemicals in our body as referenced in Chapter 4.[4] Dr. Tara Cousineau wrote an entire book about the science of compassion, titled *The Kindness Cure: How the Science of Compassion Can Heal Your Heart and Your World* (which is a must-read if you haven't done so already).

She identifies five elements of compassion:

- Acknowledging the suffering of someone else.
- Understanding that suffering is universal.
- Feeling empathy for the person suffering.

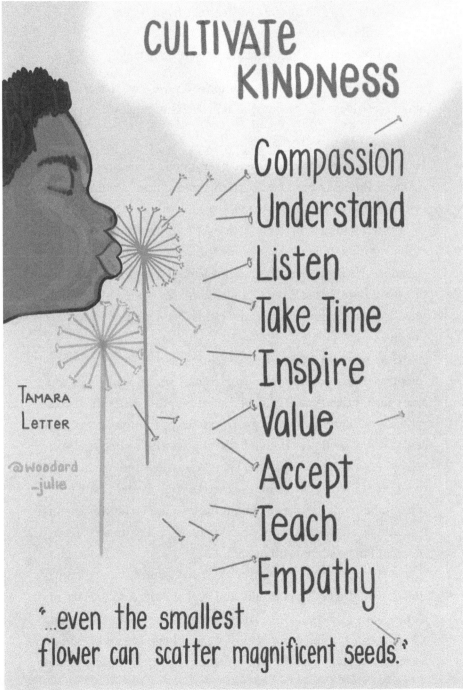

Illustration: Julie Woodard (@woodard_julie)

- Tolerating uncomfortable feelings from others and yourself.
- Taking action to relieve the person's suffering.[5]

To cultivate kindness with compassion, we have to learn more about ourselves and the ways we approach kindness with others.

U Is for Understand

Is it possible for us to understand everyone's perspective in all situations? Probably not. But to cultivate kindness, we do have to understand why people act the way they do.

I often remind myself to "seek first to understand" and avoid rushing to judgment. I don't know the complete story in a given situation and need to glean more information to make a decision or offer advice. When I try to understand someone else's point of view, it stretches my thinking and helps develop my mindset in a positive way.

Have you ever had someone respond to you sharply, without intentional provocation on your part, and you instantly feel your heart rate increase and your body temperature rise? It's a natural fight-or-flight instinct to guard ourselves in moments of perceived threat or attack. Even if I don't agree with someone else, by asking questions to learn more, I gain a broader understanding of the topic at hand while valuing someone else's thoughts and opinions. To cultivate kindness, I might need to understand a person's limitations, past experiences, or the events leading up to the exact moment I'm speaking with them.

In the past, when I found myself in a confrontational situation, I would take it personally and feel the need to protect my own actions by berating the other person's. Now I start by taking a breath and seeking a moment of mindfulness before I respond. Instead of being reactive, I'm reflective as I try to understand the other person's perspective before jumping to assumptions or judgments.

L Is for Listen

One of the easiest ways you can cultivate kindness is to listen. Not everyone will want to share their problems with the world (Nor should they!), but everyone needs someone in their life who will listen. We tell our students, "Hearing and listening are not the same thing," and it's true. To be an active listener, you need to recognize the meaning behind the words and reply in such a way that others know you are engaged in what they are sharing.

My greatest challenge with being an active listener is not interrupting someone else when they speak. As referenced before, my extended family tends to talk over one another as part of our culture, so I have to make a deliberate effort not to do this when listening to others. I recognize that others might view my interruption as a signal that my thoughts are more important than theirs, so I work harder at active listening to make sure my actions are not misunderstood. Like many, I am a constant work in progress.

When you listen to others, recognize that some people aren't looking for advice or seeking answers to a problem. Their form of mental processing might be speaking aloud. When you say, "I'm here anytime you need a listening ear," that's exactly what you are offering—a dedicated time to listen. One of the greatest gifts I received when I suffered my miscarriages was the ability to ramble about my experience with a close friend, who simply sat beside me and listened with an empathetic nod of her head.

T Is for Take Time

If you ask educators their greatest challenge in their profession, many will reference lack of time. There is never enough time to get everything done! Our lives are filled with schedules, commitments, requirements, and obligations. When do we take time for kindness?

If I want to share a smile with those passing my way, I need to take the time to look at their faces and make eye contact. If I want to surprise a coworker with a breakfast treat, I have to plan for time to make the purchase. If someone needs my assistance at work, I need to stop what I'm doing and create time where time may not exist.

Time is a precious commodity for everyone. When we realize we are no exception to this reality, time becomes a resource we all share. How we choose to use our time is what differentiates our experiences.

The older I become, the more I value time. I have to say no to some activities to say yes to others. Believe me, I am a work in progress in this area, too, and there are situations in my life when time management gets skewed in the wrong direction for the wrong reasons! I am guilty of overcommitting myself to others, which then has a negative impact on the very people I am trying to support with my time. In those moments, I give myself a little bit of grace to recalibrate and organize my time in a way that produces the greatest results for me and those around me.

Sometimes even in the midst of our busy, chaotic, never-ending to-do list, an act of kindness can provide a greater perspective of appreciation. Fourteen years after Pam Sober's mother passed away, she still grieved with a heartache that appeared to never mend. After chatting with Pam about her journey, I suggested we might do an act of kindness not only to honor her mom's legacy but to bring joy to others as well.

Together we purchased fourteen smiley-face balloons, just like the ones I bought in memory of Noah Pozner in Chapter 3. We headed to our local hospital and room-by-room we delivered the balloons to brighten the patients' days. Each year on April 27, Pam continues this tradition of kindness, adding another balloon for the current year.

When Pam discovered that my mom was in the hospital on the anniversary of her own mother's passing, she took time out of her travels to deliver one smiley-face balloon to my mom's bedside. Pam's kindness brought joy to my mom and lifted my spirits as well.

Another friend of mine, Holly Berbert, used her talents to make a special necklace for my mom when she heard she was undergoing radiation in her final days. It contained two silver charms: a small circle engraved with the word "joy" and a larger oval with the words, "I radiate." My mom wore that necklace every day she was in the hospital. It remained around her neck even when she took her last breath.

Kindness cultivators give the gift of time. They recognize that their actions matter and the time it takes to complete an act of kindness for someone else makes a difference. While we can't increase the hours in a day, we can decide how we use them to our best advantage.

I Is for Inspire

Each day is a new opportunity to inspire someone else with kindness. Have you ever been the recipient of a prepaid coffee? The idea of "suspended coffee" is when you purchase two coffees, but only consume one, leaving the remaining coffee credit to be given to someone else when they order their drink.[6] What started as a simple act of kindness inspired others to do the same, creating a ripple effect of inspiration. One year after suspended coffees were introduced, Starbucks documented more than 750 strangers purchasing coffees for people they didn't know over a two-day period.[7] Wow!

Even if you are not a coffee drinker, you can still inspire others with your kind words and actions. Maybe you hold the door open for someone, and they do the same for the person behind them. You're an inspiration! It doesn't take much to stir that same motivation in others with kindness, but we do have to make the choice to act.

Some people inspire by sharing words, while others inspire without saying anything at all. Whatever suits you, do it! The world needs your positive influence.

V Is for Value

How do we show others that we value their time, input, or assistance? With words and actions! I love the idea of dropping Anchors of Appreciation as described in *Lead Like a PIRATE: Make School Amazing for Your Students and Staff* by Shelley Burgess (@burgess_shelley) and Beth Houf (@BethHouf).[8] Imagine if we took the time to notice others, specifically mentioning something we admire or appreciate and then explaining *why*.

Talk about making somebody's day! Written notes and letters are a wonderful way to say "thank you" or show value to others. I keep my positive notes in a manila folder labeled "Smile File" and reflect back on them whenever I have a tough day. It's a great way to see yourself through someone else's eyes and remember the small things you do are noticed and appreciated.

Inspired by a Twitter post by Wendy Hankins (@MrsHankinsClass) and Kind Kids (@KindKidsAtKirk, October 19, 2018), students in our kindness classes decorated the cover of blank greeting cards to celebrate World Kindness Day on November 13. They left the inside of the card blank and added a "Created By" caption on the back with their name. Then, they placed the cards with envelopes in our school's teachers lounge so teachers could easily customize a card for a coworker, parent, or friend.

At each monthly faculty meeting, teachers pass along the Golden Apple, an apple paperweight painted with gold glitter, which is given to one staff member by the person who last received it. In announcing that month's Golden Apple award, the current recipient reveals the next winner and why that person deserves it. Each winner keeps the Golden Apple for one month before passing it on to someone else.

We also have an appreciation tradition called "Coke and a Compliment." If you know of a staff member who has been particularly helpful to you or someone else, you can grab a soda at the start of the meeting and announce who deserves the drink and why. It's always fun to learn about the kindness cultivators all around us!

Our PTA members shower us with kindness throughout the year with little treats and inspiring messages in our mailboxes.

They also keep a "Favorite Things" binder in the main office where everyone lists their favorite things, and the information is used to promote acts of kindness throughout the year. It's amazing how many times a small surprise left in a mailbox can result in perfect timing!

A Is for Accept

In cultivating kindness, we must accept others for who they are, not who we think they should be. We put so much pressure on ourselves and others to be perfect when we live in an imperfect world. No one can be happy twenty-four hours a day, 365 days a year! Even the tried-and-true Pollyannas of the world encounter moments of anguish or anger. We're all human. We make mistakes. Sometimes the most precious gift you can give someone else is acceptance.

When I give money to panhandlers on the street, I don't question what they will buy. I simply accept the fact that life is hard, and their lives are much harder than mine in that moment. I've never had to sit on a street corner asking for donations; I can't even fathom the daily challenges they endure.

Is there a chance they will use the money I give them foolishly? Yes. But I don't believe I am in a position to judge their lives, so I choose to accept their reality. Does this mean I judge you for walking by without reaching into your wallet? No. I accept that you might not share my perspective in this situation. I don't allow our differences to divide and tear apart.

Acceptance can be shown in a multitude of ways. Perhaps it's accepting someone else's apology or accepting an invitation to lunch. It might even be giving yourself a little bit of grace by accepting your own limitations in a given situation. It's important to show kindness to ourselves too.

T Is for Teach

Who taught you how to be kind? Most people first experience kindness from family members in the early days of childhood. Some had other influential people in their lives, perhaps extended family, friends, neighbors, or members of a church, synagogue, or temple. The lessons of kindness were likely simple: "Be kind to others and they will be kind to you."

While this is a wonderful sentiment, we know that kindness is not always reciprocated. It can be challenging to be kind, especially to those who are rude or hateful in return. We can't assume people instinctively know how to be kind to others.

Kindness cultivators are natural teachers because their words and actions lead the way. You don't need a formal lesson plan to make a positive difference in the life of someone else. You simply need a dedication for kindness and a willingness to share your experiences with others.

Reading children's books and novels that emphasize kindness is an excellent way to show students how to be kind. There are thousands of uplifting videos available online as well. Making a choice to teach others that kindness is important is the first step to tilling the soil.

One of my favorite teachers who cultivated kindness was George Sadler, my high school band director. He had a heart for students and an empathy that surpassed expectation. His skill at strengthening relationships created a tight-knit family, with many of those same students sharing friendships today, nearly thirty years later. Mr. Sadler taught us the importance of respecting one another despite our differences and embracing those characteristics that make us shine. I know I am a better teacher because of the seeds of kindness Mr. Sadler and others planted in me.

E Is for Empathy

When you relate to someone else's experiences as if they were your own, you develop your capacity for empathy. Sometimes it's feeling strong emotions or crying when you see someone else cry. Even babies as young as two can show empathy for others. In *UnSelfie: Why Empathetic Kids Succeed in our All-About-Me World*, Dr. Michele Borba explores the many ways empathy can be strengthened in our youth, from early childhood years through adulthood.

"If we want empathetic children, we must help them define themselves as people who care and value others, and we must instill those beliefs during childhood," she writes.[9]

Dr. Borba identifies the seven most creative ways to give children the edge they need to succeed. From being friendly to sharing their voice, children who understand empathy in themselves and others can actually take those skills and apply them to life experiences, shifting the emphasis from *me* to *we*. I highly recommend this book for any adult interested in cultivating kindness in children.

Prioritize Kindness

During a conversation with my neighbor, Julia Tyler, about the ways children learn about kindness from their families, she shared a story that resonates with her to this day:

Frequently on Sunday afternoons, Daddy would suggest visiting some elderly neighbor or relative. There hadn't yet been any leisure time on those days, as my family always went to church all morning, and we girls were required to help mama with a traditional Sunday dinner and its cleanup. By 3:00 p.m., I really wanted to be cut loose. One Sunday, I was brazen enough to speak my mind and emphatically say that I did not want to go visit any shut-ins, that I got nothing out of visiting such folks. My father's clear response has stayed with me. He said, "We are not visiting those who are housebound because of what it does for us, but for what it does for them." Daddy made it crystal clear that the main reason for kindness is the benefit of that gesture to others, not self. I shall never forget the example he set.

In our fast-paced world, it's easy to overlook opportunities for deliberate acts of kindness. Excuses will prevail if we let them. If we lose focus on the *why*, our purpose wavers and kindness is no longer a driving force in our life. During Episode 2 of her *Character Speaks* podcast,[10] Barbara Gruener discussed the topic of prioritizing kindness with Houston Kraft (@houstonkraft), co-founder of Character Strong, an organization devoted to promoting kindness and character education in the classroom.[11] Kraft identified three key reasons people hesitate to show kindness and compassion to others:

1. Incompetence—"I don't know how to do this, so I will avoid it." If someone hasn't seen or experienced kindness in action with various circumstances, or doesn't consider it a strength, they may not know how to respond when an opportunity appears. This might also include situations that make a person feel uneasy, like comforting someone who is upset if you are not emotionally inclined or not knowing what to say or do in the moment.

2. Insecurity—"I'm afraid of this, so I will avoid it." Fear is a powerful emotion of the mind that can be a challenge to overcome. Many people have fears of failure, imperfection, judgment from others, or shame. Cultivating kindness requires confidence and courage to have the greatest impact. You can overcome insecurity by recognizing when those feelings take hold of your heart and making efforts to overcome them.

3. Inconvenience—"I don't have time" or "I don't feel like it." Much like Julia's story above, kindness may feel like an imposition, especially when done out of obligation or expectation. Finding the joy in sharing kindness with others shifts the perspective from inconvenience to priority.

Recognizing opportunities for kindness—and our responses to those moments—is the first step to strengthening our own social-emotional learning. "Some people think social-emotional learning or character education is another thing added to their plate," Houston said. "I believe it *is* the plate. We have to build the foundation first."[12]

Kris Jenkins (@PreK33), an early childhood educator in Hutchinson, Kansas, cultivates kindness as the chair of the community giving committee for her local philanthropic educational organization (P.E.O.). In addition to expanding the group's signature cause of giving books to multiple grade levels, she has created a list of suggested donations members can bring to monthly meetings. Items such as T-shirts, coats, and hygiene products then get distributed throughout their community. The volunteer organization also raises funds for grants, scholarships, and loans for college assistance.

For more information about P.E.O., visit peointernational.org.

When my childhood friend Laura Jones was battling stage four colon cancer, she was hesitant at first to reach out for help. "I hate being an imposition," she told me as she sat in my living room, rocking my newborn son. "I much prefer giving than receiving." I can understand that sentiment all too well! There are times when it's much easier to give than to receive, but in declining someone's offer of help, we can rob that person of an opportunity to experience joy through giving.

During Laura's cancer battle, we blessed her by planting flowers she could see from the windows in her home. It was a small act of prioritizing kindness, but one that had a significant impact as her health deteriorated and she spent more time inside.

When my friend, Justin Birckbichler (@absotTC), discovered he had testicular cancer, he documented his journey on his website,[13] using the platform to advocate for men's health and share stories about the kindness he received from others. He even shared insight on what *not* to say to a cancer patient, guiding others in the impact of their kind words.[14]

Kindness at Home

In the winter, my husband starts my car before I leave for work and makes a fresh pot of coffee in the morning because he knows I hate being cold. He takes care of all the yard work, empties the trash, and manages the bills. He helps to coordinate the pick-ups when one child is at daycare and the other has after-school activities. He chats with our neighbors when he sees them outside, even though he is a self-labeled introvert. He even volunteers his weekend time as a coach for the Sports Backers Marathon Training Team, which requires a commitment of time and dedication to assist others in their personal goals.

Some might argue that these are not acts of kindness, but I would disagree! Anytime you do something nice for someone else—because you know it will have a positive impact on their lives—is an act of kindness! It's all in how we choose to view the world around us. Are we pouring out or filling up? Do we see responsibility or opportunity? When we shift perspective of the power of our impact, we start to see a multitude of ways we can make someone else's day brighter through simple acts of service.

My father-in-law invites us out to breakfast and offers to watch the kids when our schedules conflict. He even bakes sweet treats for me to bring to school to share with other teachers throughout the week. His enthusiasm for kind acts is contagious!

Tilling the soil in ourselves and others provides a fertile space for cultivating kindness. Prioritizing kindness in our lives makes us more aware of ways we can lift others and make a direct impact on how they feel.

Kindness Cultivator Spotlight

Melanie Korach

#StarfishClub
Twitter: @melanie_korach
Instagram: @melaniekorach

The Starfish Club is a kindness movement created by Melanie Korach, a teacher with the Durham District School Board in Whitby, Ontario, Canada. Inspired by the starfish story written by Loren Eiseley, the club embodies the mindset that every act of kindness is important, no matter how small. With just about 10,000 participants worldwide since its start in December 2017, the Starfish Club continues to inspire people daily through their hashtag #StarfishClub. "We can do our part to change the world and make a difference by helping people, supporting each other in chasing our dreams, and turning random acts of kindness into an essential part of our daily way of life."

Melanie and her teaching partner engage students with weekly starfish challenges that include reflections in starfish diaries. For older elementary students, they created a Junior Starfish Club to include writing kindness poems and sharing inspiring quotes.

Other classes have joined in the fun of sharing kindness, creating a boomerang effect as kindness is returned to them as well. Weekly meetings help to continue the passion for kindness beyond the school walls and into the community. They've even had their poetry displayed at a police station in England! "The quiet ripples we make, when combined together, create transformation," Melanie says. "The ultimate goal of Starfish Club members is to provide more peace and happiness to each other and to the world as a whole."

To learn more about Melanie Korach's passion
for kindness, favorite kindness quotes, and more,
visit tamaraletter.com.

Points to Ponder

 What are your earliest memories of kindness? How have those experiences impacted the person you are today?

 Of the nine characteristics to CULTIVATE kindness, which are your strengths? Which would you like to develop more?

What are your favorite ways to show kindness to others in the workplace or at home?

Chapter 8

Planting Seeds

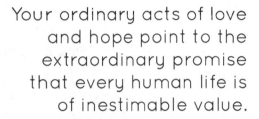

Your ordinary acts of love
and hope point to the
extraordinary promise
that every human life is
of inestimable value.

—Desmond Tutu

I have a confession to make—one I'm slightly embarrassed to admit, especially with the theme of this section. If I share my confession, will you promise to not judge my vulnerability? OK, here it is:

I am a horrible gardener.

There. I said it. Now I can stop holding my breath, wondering if my hidden secret will be uncovered when I least expect it. I just admitted one of my weaknesses to the world!

Although I love cultivating kindness, sowing actual plant seeds and nurturing them to germination is a skill I have yet to master. I have tried, multiple times, but either the plant grows for a bit and then dies or simply never sprouts at all. I'm always faced with questions when growth is stagnant. *Did I provide the plant with ample sunlight and water? Is the seed pushed into the soil deep enough to take root? Do I have the right soil and temperate conditions to match my plant's needs?* All my attempts at growing and sustaining plant life have failed.

Despite my lack of horticultural strengths, I have always been mesmerized by contrasts of nature shown through my travels and in books I read. In my youth, I was drawn to *A Tree Grows in Brooklyn* by Betty Smith. I stumbled across this book, quite literally, as a thirteen-year-old visiting my local library, my attention on the shelves, not the floor. After tripping over this object in my path, the title intrigued me, as did the description on the inside cover: "A story of tears and laughter, cruelty and compassion, so crowded with life and people that no description can begin to convey its spell."[1]

My heart pounded as I instantly felt a connection to this book, despite its copyright date decades before. How could a tree grow in a city and what did that have to do with cruelty and compassion? I picked up the book from the floor, tucked it under my arm to check out, and spent the remainder of my summer reading.

I connected to the protagonist, Francie Nolan, in a way I had never connected to a literary character before. She was eleven years old when her story began in 1912, and by the final chapter of the book I had followed Francie's journey into adulthood. Through these pages, I saw glimpses of diversity, developed an insatiable urge to help the underdog, and realized the power of words to whisk me away from my own trials and tribulations.

In the first chapter of *A Tree Grows in Brooklyn*, Betty Smith describes the tree growing in Francie's yard, which would become a symbol of survival throughout the book:

Some people called it the Tree of Heaven. No matter where its seed fell, it made a tree which struggled to reach the sky. It grew in

boarded-up lots and out of neglected rubbish heads, and it was the only tree that grew out of cement.[2]

The paradox struck me to the core. A single seed, one not even planted in nutrient-rich soil, somehow managed to grow despite the conditions surrounding it. How could this be possible?

Maximizing Mindset

Jimmy Casas reminds us in his book, *Culturize: Every Student. Every Day. Whatever It Takes*, that "no one person is responsible for determining your success or failure but you, and no one is responsible for your morale but you."[3] In reflecting on my lackluster success in gardening, it would be easy to give up and consider myself a failure. I could view other gardeners with envy and complain about their success while bemoaning the woe-is-me sorrows of my own experiences. I might even be tempted to undermine the talents of a skilled horticulturist, simply to make my meager attempts shine brighter, or blame the plant itself for choosing not to grow!

But what if I chose to maximize my mindset and take ownership for my failure? Could I still have value by admitting that I'm not the best gardener? Would it be possible for me to shift my perspective away from me and onto others, finding unique ways to support, encourage, and uplift those who had found success? What if I chose fortitude over failure?

In education, we constantly see the pendulum swing with new priorities, new programs, new perspectives. While academic content mastery remains a priority in much of what we teach, social and emotional learning (SEL) skills are receiving greater attention for those foundational supports that help students learn and grow. The Collaborative for Academic, Social, and Emotional Learning (CASEL) provides five core competencies for SEL supports:

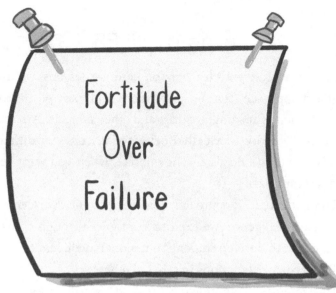

Illustration: Julie Woodard (@woodard_julie)

- Self-Awareness
- Self-Management
- Responsible Decision-Making
- Relationship Skills
- Social Awareness[4]

What I love about this model is the emphasis on helping even our youngest students learn about themselves and others as they work with school, home, and community partnerships to shape their journey into adulthood. Our challenge is to find ways we can mesh these life lessons in the parameters of our daily instruction, thus saving time and promoting relevancy.

To learn more about SEL and access hundreds of resources, visit casel.org.

Using a RULER

When I collaborate with teachers on kindness lessons, we use an integrated approach, sharing discussions and examples through the integration of reading, writing, and other subjects. After reading *Those Shoes* by Maribeth Boelts, we discuss the difference between wants and needs and how it feels when you want something you can't have.

Using the RULER approach, developed by the Yale Center for Emotional Intelligence, we explore key topics through conversation that help to develop students' emotional intelligence:

R—Recognize emotions in self and others

U—Understand emotional causes and consequences

L—Label emotions accurately

E—Express emotions accurately

R—Regulate emotions effectively[5]

This discussion naturally leads to questions about acts of kindness and how we feel when we give or receive kindness from others. Most student responses are positive, but a few showcase the complexities of emotions we feel when we step outside of our comfort zone:

- "It feels weird receiving something when I don't have anything to share in return."
- "If someone gives me a compliment, I don't know what to say."
- "When I think about doing something nice for someone else, my stomach feels all fluttery. What if they don't like what I do?"

Sometimes I'm amazed how similar children and adults are with their feelings. I have to remind students that I have those same feelings too! By sharing my own vulnerabilities in being kind to others, trust and respect is added to that beautiful tapestry of learning, allowing us to have deeper conversations into ways we can plant seeds of kindness in others.

Words of Inspiration

"What would you like to do to improve the school?"

Debbie Arco, former principal and curriculum and instruction director with Hanover County Public Schools, believes in the power of choice and voice. "If you want students to take pride in their school and community, you must give them an opportunity to share their thoughts and feelings."[6]

She created a middle school leadership team, selecting students from all social groups throughout the school with diverse interests, backgrounds, and strengths. They met regularly to discuss solutions to various issues, then transformed their ideas into actions.

One project that developed from this team was repainting the bathroom walls to include positive messages promoting the school's pillars of character. Students chose the phrases, colors, and themes, then worked together to transform the sterile restrooms into places that were warm and welcoming, with the end goal to prevent repeated graffiti and promote positivity.

It worked! Students took pride and ownership of their transformed space and repainting was no longer an issue to solve.

Jay Billy (@JayBilly2), principal with Lawrence Township Public Schools and author of *Lead with Culture: What Really Matters in Our Schools*, used his school's staircases as canvases for promoting positive culture. On each stair step was written a specific mindset phrase that students could read as they walked to the next floor.

Photo Credit: Jay Billy (@JayBilly2)

When you
Enter this
Loving School
Consider yourself
One of the special
Members of an
Extraordinary Family

#KindnessMatters

Photo Credit: Jay Billy (@JayBilly2)

#Kindness Matters

Photo Credit: Jay Billy (@JayBilly2)

Jay also shined a light on kindness (Literally!) as he displayed illuminated messages of kindness on classroom windows for the community to see, even in the darkness. They even brightened up a dull green storage container with reminders of kindness.

At the entrance of their school, a welcome message was painted on the stoop:

When you
Enter this
Loving school,
Consider yourself
One of the special
Members of an
Extraordinary family!

It's exciting when we see messages of kindness go viral on the internet and show up across social media platforms that are then brought into our schools and communities. One of my favorite messages was created in the form of a letter from Bryan Skavnak, author of *Happy Golf Starts Here,* to his golfing students:

Some kids are smarter than you,
Some kids have cooler clothes than you,
Some kids are better at sports than you.
It doesn't matter.
You have your thing, too.
Be the kid who can get along.
Be the kid who is generous.
Be the kid who is happy for other people.
Be the kid who does the right thing.
Be the nice kid.[7]

Imagine my delight when I discovered this exact phrase painted on a wall in my child's middle school! Every single day, my son is reminded of the importance of being nice. As a parent, this one act of intentional purpose means more than his principal, Mr. Mark Beckett, will ever know. This visual reminder at Chickahominy Middle School encourages students to recognize the value in being the nice kid.

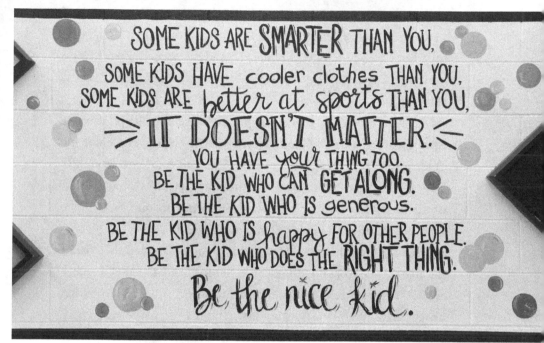

Artwork: Kristin Donaldson Photo Credit: Lisa Zader, CapturedbytheLens.com

Buddy Benches

For many elementary students, recess is the highlight of their day. The opportunity to run around a blacktop, swing on swings, or play a game with friends is a welcome break from listening and learning. For some children, however, recess is a dreaded chore. They don't enjoy physical activity like their peers or don't always have someone to play with on the playground. Because recess time is one of the most social times in a student's day, the latter can be devastating.

In 2013, a first-grade student named Christian Bucks introduced the concept of a Buddy Bench to his elementary school "to eliminate loneliness and foster friendship on the playground . . . to allow others to meet and play with old friends or new friends."[8] If a student sits on a designated Buddy Bench, it's a silent signal that they want to be included in play. This idea sparked a worldwide movement, with hundreds of schools now offering a Buddy Bench at recess.

This idea of Buddy Benches planted a seed of inspiration in April Roberts, a cosmetology teacher at The Hanover Center for Trades and Technology (THCTT). She and students from the Hanover County Public School's Student Advisory Council asked if our district could provide Buddy Benches to our elementary schools. Our district leadership readily agreed.

Each school that wanted a Buddy Bench provided the cost of the materials. Working with Jamie Sanford, a carpentry teacher at THCTT, high school students got to work building ten buddy benches for elementary students. The words "Buddy Bench" were carved into each wooden bench and personalized with the school's abbreviation.

Cosmetology students painted the benches a brilliant shade of blue and decorated them with their handprints in a variety of colors before each bench was delivered to the schools.[9]

The concept of a Buddy Bench was planted with seeds of kindness, but the success is rooted in a school's culture. How the bench is introduced and used during recess time might vary from place to place. In a school where the expectation is to be kind to others, you might see an increased awareness and acceptance as the bench becomes a social magnet, connecting those without friends or playmates to others who are willing to offer inclusion.

Photo Credit: Lisa Zader, CapturedbytheLens.com

In a school environment that prides itself on its competitive nature or doesn't take the time to cultivate empathy in others, the purpose might never reach its positive potential. *What happens when students sit on a Buddy Bench in that type of school culture? Will those children be teased because nobody wants to play with them? Will drawing attention to their loneliness add more if no one asks them to play? If a teacher sits beside them, will they be viewed as a teacher's pet?*

It takes courage for students to sit at a Buddy Bench. They are saying to every other child on the playground, "I'm lonely and need a friend to play." Depending on their emotional maturity, they might intentionally avoid the Buddy Bench so as not to draw even more attention to themselves for being alone.

Some students don't have a desire to play with others. They're content to spend recess reading a favorite book or drawing in a journal. It's important not to assume that all students want to join in the same activities. Learning more about our students helps us distinguish when someone is feeling content or alone.

Would you like to know more about Buddy Benches? Follow Christian's adventures on his Facebook Page! facebook.com/buddybenches.

Whether or not your school has a designated Buddy Bench, it's important for adults to pay attention to social dynamics as students interact and play. Look to see who plays alone and who plays in groups. Does this match their personalities in class or at home? How are their friendships shifting? How do they grapple with decision-making and conflict resolution? There are times when we need to step aside and allow students to work through issues on their own and other times when we need to intervene to set the example. We must never assume children have mastered the art of social engagement.

In older grades, where unstructured outdoor play is not an option, it's just as important to be aware of social dynamics in the classroom, cafeteria, hallways, and school bus. Clubs and extra-curricular activities provide a social breeding ground for developing and strengthening relationships but can also be a battlefield for the excluded or shunned student. It's our duty as educators to recognize shifts in social culture and reach out to those students who might be struggling.

Even as adults, we plant seeds of kindness by modeling the behaviors we want to see in others. Similar to the concept of a Buddy Bench, we might go out of our way to seek out others who are alone or off to the side. Do you know someone who eats alone in their room or cubicle? Offer to join them for lunch or invite them to your space to eat. Do you know a coworker who works only the mandated hours of the time clock, nothing more, always rushing out when the day is done? She could be struggling to make a connection with your school and might feel like she doesn't fit in. Or maybe she has a second job or small children to care for after work. Start a conversation, and get to know these people not just as coworkers, but also as individuals with value, purpose, and interests. Asking a question might crack open the door of isolation, making a connection that could be a lifeline.

Planting seeds of kindness means taking time and stepping out of our comfort zones, just as we expect others to do the same. It means taking a risk that our kindness might be rejected. Is it worth that risk?

Absolutely. Take the risk.

Kindness Cultivator Spotlight

Kate Lapetino

#FieldKindness

Twitter: @kcmgd31

Website: sites.google.com/ccsd21.org/fieldkindness

Fourth-grade teacher Kate Lapetino brings kindness into her classroom each and every day. With a year-long focus on kindness woven into thirteen separate initiatives, her passion for kindness knows no bounds!

Kate began a Weekly Kindness Challenge in her school to see if fourth graders could spread their kindness beyond the walls of Eugene Field Elementary School in Wheeling, Illinois. Each week students were provided a new act of kindness to perform such as donating items or giving a stranger a compliment. By the end of the school year, the fourth graders in her school had completed more than thirty-four hundred random acts of kindness!

In addition to the Weekly Kindness Challenge, students also participated in World Kindness Day (November 13), Random Acts of Kindness Day (February 17), and aligned kindness activities with other holidays throughout the year. They created kindness videos, designed encouraging notes to place on middle school students' lockers, played games with senior citizens, packed individual care bags for a local shelter, and distributed more than seven hundred compostable seed papers for others to plant in celebration of Earth Day.

Their initiatives have scattered globally, thanks to social media. Using the hashtag #FieldKindness, they have shared more than two hundred posts documenting their kindness journey, many of which have been liked or shared by other kindness cultivators around the world. They even experienced several pay-it-forward moments, with Leon Logothetis (*The Kindness Diaries*) donating one hundred books for one hundred postcards created, and Michael's stores donating more than one hundred hospital gowns valued at twenty-five dollars each for every student-designed hospital gown submitted to their My Starlight Gown contest.

Kate's advice for cultivating kindness is simple. "Don't let it become a 'one-and-done' project. Truly make a change in mindset and habits by spreading kindness and talking about kindness often."

To learn more about Kate Lapetino's passion for kindness, favorite kindness quotes, and more, visit tamaraletter.com.

Points to Ponder

 How are you planting seeds of kindness in your classroom, workplace, home, or community?

What are your favorite words of inspiration?

In what ways could social and emotional learning impact what you do each day?

Chapter 9

Roots and Stems

Too often we underestimate
the power of a touch, a smile,
a kind word, a listening ear,
an honest compliment, or
the smallest act of caring, all
of which have the potential
to turn a life around.

—Leo Buscaglia

Taraxacum originale is a special type of flower that has unique characteristics. It's one of the only flowers that is completely edible: petals, roots, and stems. They are found on all seven continents and have been used for medicinal purposes for several generations. The tap root of *Taraxacum originale* can stretch to one-and-a-half feet through the soil, providing exceptional stability as it grows. Each day its bright yellow petals open with the daylight and close as night appears. When the time comes for seed dispersal, the yellow petals form a white puffball that, with the help of the wind, will scatter more than two hundred seeds for miles.[1]

What is this amazing, hearty plant that is labeled a nuisance by many? *Taraxacum originale* is best known by its common name— *dandelion* or *dent-de-lion* in French, referencing the lion's-tooth shape of its leaves.[2] What astounds me most about this weed is its ability to regenerate and persevere despite continual attempts to eradicate it from a front lawn.

Imagine for a moment that our words and actions are like those dandelion seeds. With one simple action, our seeds of kindness scatter with the wind, landing and blooming with minimal assistance from others. Each small seed grows a single dandelion plant, only to have that plant produce hundreds of additional seeds, to scatter and continue the cycle again.

Think of the impact of your kindness. It's truly endless!

When you cultivate kindness, the power is in your roots and stems. The roots spread, unnoticed, without fanfare, yet become the lifeline of your existence. As your stem sprouts and grows, it becomes taller and stronger, with the ability to withstand a variety of seasonal changes and storms that come your way. You've tilled the soil and planted your seeds. Now is the time to grow.

Stagnant Seeds

In the classroom, there will be times when you might feel like a frustrated farmer: You have modified conditions for optimal growth, you've planted the seeds in nutrient-rich soil, and have provided adequate water and light. You wait. And wait. And wait. Chances are your patience will wane as you start to doubt the work of your cultivation. *Was it the soil? The location? What went wrong? Why didn't this seed grow?*

What you can't see are all the ways those seeds are transforming from the inside out. Not all seeds grow at the same rate or the same way. Some have shallow roots, and others spread far and wide before the first sign of life appears above the soil.

Keep sowing.

Theodore Roosevelt once said, "Comparison is the thief of joy." While his comment was not referencing plant growth per se, the analogy is valid across a range of circumstances. Why do we compare the growth of one person against another when we know people grow and develop at different rates? Even under identical circumstances, there will always be a deviation from expected results.

Keep sowing.

Your seeds are planted. Stop comparing their progress. The reality is, you might not see growth from one seed until the end of the year or never at all. Does that mean that one seed will never sprout for someone else to enjoy, that all that effort was a waste of time?

Keep sowing.

Some seeds bloom late according to the timeline on a calendar page, but those same seeds might bloom exactly on time according to their development. Roots and stems are indicators that growth is happening. Be patient. Give it time. The blooms will come when you least expect it.

Keep sowing.

See the Unseen

"Which comes first—the roots or the stem?" I have posed this question to students countless times as I have taught the plant life cycle, and most, if not all, answer a similar way. First the seed is planted, then the roots grow. Finally, the stem appears followed by a flower. Simple enough.

But planting seeds of kindness and watching them germinate to full bloom is *not* so simple. It takes time. It takes patience. It takes an unwavering belief that the work you do in tilling the soil and planting the seed is actually taking root in the foundation to produce a strong and healthy environment that will eventually scatter seeds of its own. In many cases, we are not the ones who get to enjoy the final blooms.

I used to think kindness was a "soft skill." Its importance in my direct instruction took a backseat to state-mandated topics such as reading, writing, math, science, and social studies. That's not to say those topics are unworthy of our time; oh no, quite the opposite! We must teach and strengthen curricular knowledge in our students, so their learning can expand and connect to other more complex topics of understanding as their brains develop and mature. If our instruction contains only these basics of learning, however, we are short-changing our students and robbing our future.

Illustration: Julie Woodard (@woodard_julie)

We are in the business of raising people. We are in the business of shaping culture and molding the next generation of citizens in this world. Each of us has a role to play, whether teacher, specialist, counselor, administrator, parent, community member, or friend. The opportunity to change the world is right here in front of us each and every day!

We must take time to let those roots grow, even when we can't see the work below the surface. We must keep the foundation fertile and ripe for new growth and trust the process. Strong roots create tenacity and perseverance to reach and stretch and create new paths of nourishment. The question is, how do we strengthen roots when they grow below the surface?

We make a choice to see the unseen.

In Chapter 1, I described my experience of being the new kid in town. At the age of eight, I was uprooted from all I had known and replanted in new soil. It was a time of extreme vulnerability, but, thankfully, I was too young to realize the impact of such change.

My first task for survival in a new school was to find a friend. As an extrovert, you would think this would have been easy for me, but within minutes of entering the classroom, other students had labeled me according to their preconceived judgments of my appearance. *I was short. I had glasses. I had freckles. Therefore, I was dumb. Not worth their time.*

Did my classmates *really* think I was dumb and not worth their time? Maybe, maybe not. But those are the words that bore into my heart that year because that's what I heard others whisper about me. It took years to dull their impact, and even today I cringe when I hear other students negatively talk about their classmates.

Roots are hardy and, when faced with obstructions, they will grow in different directions. The same happens with us as well. Throughout my third-grade year, I met other kids in my class who showed kind hearts, and many of those friendships continue to this day.

At an early age, I made a commitment to see the unseen, but I will admit that there were times when my words or actions might have been cruel as I grappled with the social shunning that occurs from being brave. It's easy to be mean; it's much harder to be kind, especially when there are direct ramifications from others.

Kindness is a choice. Plain and simple. You can choose to be kind or not. Just like Auggie discovered in the book *Wonder*, by R. J. Palacio, choosing to be kind when you are being teased, taunted, and even bullied is challenging. It takes a strong support system to overcome unkind, even hateful, people.

Peacemakers

Who receives rank on your ladder of trust? Is there a special friend, neighbor, or family member you turn to when the seas are rough and murky? Who do you confide in when you are greeted with the wrongs of the world?

For many years, my grandma was my anchor in the sea of chaos and change. When I arrived at her house on Sundays, it was always to a hot meal, a warm smile, and a listening ear. She was my safe harbor when life became too difficult to navigate.

Not everyone has a Grandma Payne, however, and for those whose lives are tumultuous at best, growing strong roots can be extremely challenging. I think about the students who have entered my classroom only to leave again before the school year ended. Transiency is a great hindrance to children and teenagers trying to develop consistent support systems. How do we create environments that are mindful of this?

We seek out the peacemakers.

Peacemakers are those helpers who consistently look for the good in people and situations. They are the calming antidote to a chaotic world. They seek change in positive ways and show respect, kindness, and courage in all they do. They show empathy and embrace compassion for others. We find them in our classrooms. We discover them in our workplaces. We learn about them from others.

Martin Luther King, Jr., chose to see the unseen in a time of great oppression and rose with strength and dignity to help those whose voices were silenced. He defended the rights of all people and became an iconic example of love, kindness, and acceptance. While his life ended before mine even began, his legacy of love and kindness lives on in the lives of those around me. Each year I am privileged to spotlight him and other peacemakers throughout our curriculum as we share stories of their courage to be the good.

Another peacemaker was Fred Rogers, who asked children of all ages, "Won't you be my neighbor?" He, too, understood the importance of finding a friend and creating a support system in others. As a young boy, he grappled with the negative events in the world, and his mother would say, "Look for the helpers. You will always find people who are helping."[3]

Look around at those you encounter each day. Can you find the helpers, the peacemakers? Who inspires you to be kind, compassionate, understanding? Perhaps you are a peacemaker for someone else!

You've Got a Friend

Long before cell phones and email, I would spend my summers writing letters to the new friends I met on vacations and school trips. I remember anxiously waiting for the daily visit of my mail carrier, and running out to check my mailbox to see if a reply might be delivered. Oh, the joy of receiving a letter in return! I would read and reread their handwritten stories as I learned more about my new connections. Although our paths might never cross again, I still considered them treasured friends.

Even before the age of social media, I was blooming into a social butterfly. I openly welcomed friendship from a variety of social groups; if you were kind to me, I would show kindness in return. Having people in my network that I trusted provided safety in vulnerability, as I knew they would always be there to pick me up whenever I fell down.

Adults are no different from children in this way. We all need a PLN. Whether a close best friend or a crew of many, knowing you have someone in your corner to cheer you on and lift you higher makes the challenges of this world a bit easier to bear.

Creating a strong support system of friendship is like strengthening the root system underground. It helps us stand a bit taller and keeps our foundation intact when the winds of change try to blow us over. Without friends, our world is narrow and thin, making it even harder to withstand the negative things that eventually come our way.

Bestie or Bully?

When you look back at your childhood, is it through the lens of hazy nostalgia or jaded scorn? I think for many of us we have moments of both, though we may favor one perspective over the other. It seems the older I become, the more painful moments appear fuzzy around the edges, leaving me with a false sense of childhood perfection. "Back when I was a kid . . ." stories receive a groan from my own children because they know whatever story I have to share won't match their realities of today.

As mentioned before, many of my childhood memories were captured in my diary where I wrote about daily life. My diary was raw and real, as only a teenager can describe, and the stories kept inside are a great reminder to me as an older adult that my picture-perfect memories of childhood were actually quite challenging and brutal at times.

I wrote about my besties, those friends who were in the inner circle of friendship, who formed my root system in childhood. I also wrote about bullies.

My first encounter with a bully was not on that pivotal day of third grade when I started a new school. No, those classmates were just being mean, and their snide remarks eased up as the days and weeks continued. It wasn't until a few years later that I came face-to-face with a true bully: a tall girl we'll call Jean.

Everyone wanted to be friends with Jean. Not because she was pretty or popular, but because she had power. If you were on her good side, she left you alone. If you were on her bad side, she made it her personal mission to destroy you in every way possible.

Jean's favorite place to hang out was the entrance of the girl's restroom. She would linger inside, around the first corner, out of view from someone passing down the hall. She reminded me of those terrifying clowns that hide in the shadows, then jump out at you in the darkened alleys of a haunted house attraction at the state fair.

But this wasn't a haunted house. This was school. My safe place. The place that provided consistency and stability to balance out the unpredictability of my home life. The place where I was supposed to learn and grow, not add to my fear and apprehension.

If Jean was in a good mood, she would simply say something degrading to you as you walked in the restroom. If she was in a bad mood, she would threaten you as you walked in and torment you with hateful comments through the stall door as you tried to take care of business as quickly as possible. Sometimes she charged you money as you entered. I remember asking my mom for extra lunch money to buy ice cream that I actually used to pay Jean so I could use the restroom. I finally ran out of extra money and stopped using the restroom during the day.

Awareness and Accountability

In *Dare to Be Kind: How Extraordinary Compassion Can Transform Our World*, Lizzie Velasquez defines a bully as "someone who uses their strength, whether physical, verbal, or emotional, to hurt or intimidate someone else they perceive as being weaker than themselves."[4] Lizzie knows firsthand the horrors of cyberbullying: she discovered a video of herself on YouTube posted by a stranger titled, "World's Ugliest Woman" with hundreds of hateful, degrading comments for the world to see. Her story as the target of vile and detestable judgment shows not only the pain and heartbreak of being an unsuspecting victim, but also the grace and perseverance to overcome negativity with kindness and compassion.

Bullying is prevalent across our country and around the world. The United States Centers for Disease Control (CDC) and the Department of Education (DOE) identify modes and types of bullying for school-aged children:

Modes and Types of Bullying

Modes	Types
• Direct • Indirect	• Physical • Verbal • Relational • Damage to Property

Information courtesy of stopbullying.gov/media/facts/index.html

While bullying can happen any time, any place, cyberbullying, or bullying through an electronic platform, can include anything from verbal exchanges to modifying and destroying privately stored digital information. Criminal charges can be filed against those who bully others to include harassment, hazing, and assault.[5] When responding to bullying, the two most critical elements are awareness and immediate action.

The term "bullying" has seen an increase in media attention, particularly in relation to teen suicide. It is a complex issue that deserves continued, honest discussion and action. According to the CDC, from the years 2000 to 2016, the suicide rate among men ages ten to twenty-four increased 16 percent while the suicide rate among women of the same age increased by 50 percent.[6] We must remove the stigma of bullying so our children are empowered to rise tall in the face of adversity, knowing their root system will keep them safe and strong.

When I was bullied in the school restroom, I felt helpless to tell anyone. It was common knowledge that if Jean found out that you tattled on her, there would be worse payment than some change at the doorway. The fear and intimidation were enough to keep my mouth shut.

Bullies like Jean knew they had the upper hand because silence was their sanctuary. They exerted power like an invisible sword that could cut you in two. I was one of the lucky ones. I escaped my bully through avoidance. I was not tormented day and night.

Back then, teachers rarely discussed topics like bullying, social relationships, or even kindness, for that matter. In the early elementary years, they might share a picture book or two, but the older we became, the emphasis on tough topics and social discourse faded into the background, and the focus settled on academic achievement. Bullying was something you might discuss with friends, but rarely adults; you had to figure it out for yourself.

Today's culture is not the same as the one of my childhood, and I would bet it's not the same as yours either. Children now have instant access to the world around them, which creates additional challenges in shaping who they are and who they will become.

We must be the change. We need to keep these topics at the forefront of our instruction, as we interact with children daily who struggle under the weight of this oppression. Although bullying is most prevalent in middle school, one in four students in the United States reports having been bullied during childhood.[7] Does this mean bullying isn't prevalent in other schools, in other countries? Absolutely not! What this data does show, however, is that bullying is still an issue in our schools and needs to be addressed past elementary school.

What makes the bullying issue even more complicated for children, parents, and teachers is the prevalence of cyberbullying. According to the *Journal of Aggression, Maltreatment, and Trauma*, cyberbullying is defined as the "willful and repeated harm inflicted through the use of computers, cell phones, and other electronic devices."[9] In a study of more than 2,700 students ages eleven to seventeen, there was an overlapping relationship between school bullying and cyberbullying, increasing the need for continued conversation and intervention from teachers, administrators, and parents regarding these topics.[10]

The ease of access to digital devices in young children is astounding. Findings from the Nielsen's Fourth-Quarter 2016 Mobile Kids Report of children ages six through twelve show the predominant age of children receiving their first cell phone is the age of ten, with 81 percent indicating their top mobile activity as text messaging.[11] In our classroom lessons where students are taught the nuances of written communication, are we addressing the relevant need for acceptable use on and off the digital grid?

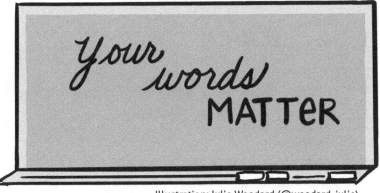

Illustration: Julie Woodard (@woodard_julie)

Our children are forced to tackle digital social issues that didn't exist ten or twenty years ago. As teachers and parents, we often feel helpless to guide our children through these murky waters, as our own understanding of these complexities is limited to personal experiences. Common Sense Media is an excellent resource for additional information and support including app and website reviews, research articles, and parent resources. In their article, "It's Not Cyberbullying, but . . ." Christine Elgersma identifies eight key areas of negative digital interactions:

- Ghosting
  Cutting off online communication and avoiding response

- Subtweeting
  Tweeting or posting negatively about someone else without mentioning them by name or tagging them

- Fake Accounts
  Creating a new account under a different name and posting from that account to stir up trouble or divert attention

- Sharing embarrassing posts and pics
  Posting candid photos with cruel captions

- Rumors
  Posting fake news as fact

- Exclusion
  Posting photos and/or descriptions of group activities knowing an excluded friend will view it

- Griefing
  In a gaming environment, deliberately causing havoc to another (swiping coins/materials, deliberately killing other characters, harassing others in a chat)

- Hate Speech
  Targeted language directed to a person or group based on personal traits such as race, religion, disability, ethnicity, nationality, sexual orientation, gender identity, or belief system[12]

What sets hate speech apart from cyberbullying is the frequency of the action; however, all of these can have a traumatic impact on children and those who form their social groups. With the additional layer of cyberbullying, lives can be affected twenty-four hours a day, seven days a week. The social stigma attached to cyberbullying is constant, pervasive, and brutal. We must be vigilant in listening to our children and taking their concerns seriously. We must also be mindful of those who are suffering silently in our midst. It is our duty to keep our children safe even when they are not under our direct care. We must teach our students to be kind, but to also understand that safety is a higher priority.

To learn more about Common Sense Media,
visit commonsensemedia.org.

Stems of Strength

Why do some children bully others? In *Dare to Be Kind*, Lizzie answers that question with such simplicity it can break your heart: "Hurt people hurt people."[13] *Psychology Today* identifies four key characteristics that might make someone prone to become a target of a bully:

- Being Different
- Being Competent
- Being Nice
- Being Isolated[14]

It's tough being kind sometimes! We need to empower our students to not only stand up for themselves, but to stand up for others they see bullied as well. Jennifer Casa-Todd reminds us in her book, *Social LEADia*, that while it is tempting to go head-to-head with a bully, especially in an emotionally charged moment of anger or frustration, responding with compassion to the person being bullied, either publicly or privately, will help to build up that person and remind them of their value.[15]

Lizzie takes this mindset of empathy even further:

Fighting anger with anger does nothing but make the problem bigger . . . I wish everyone could recognize, instantly and deeply, that no matter what awful things are said or done to them, they should not take it personally, because it has nothing to do with them.[16]

Lizzie chooses to offer compassion directly to those who have bullied her, but admits that it took a very long time to be brave enough to follow through with action. With intentionality, kindness is now her automatic mindset when faced with hurtful words or actions by others.

As an educator and a mom, my pulse races anytime I discuss bullying with children or adults. I wish I could wave a magic wand to remove bullying from our lives completely, or at least have a perfect answer to give others when they ask, "What should I do?" I want children to be upstanders, not bystanders, but each bullying situation is different and paradoxically the same: power and control are always at the forefront.

To decrease, and eventually stop, bullying over a period of time, adults need to respond quickly and consistently. This sends the message that bullying will not be tolerated and is not acceptable behavior. Specific responses might vary in different locations, but stopbullying.gov makes the following recommendations:

DO

- Intervene immediately.
- Get assistance from another adult if necessary.
- Separate those involved.
- Verify safety for individuals.
- Meet immediate medical or mental health needs.
- Stay calm.
- Reassure individuals and bystanders.
- Model respectful behavior.

DON'T

- Ignore bullying.
- Assume children can work through bullying on their own.
- Immediately try to sort out facts.
- Force others to state publicly what they saw or heard.
- Question individuals involved in front of bystanders.
- Talk to individuals involved together, only separately.
- Make individuals involved apologize to others on the spot.

There might be times where immediate medical help or police assistance is necessary during or after an altercation. Seek out additional support if bullying includes any of the following:

- A weapon
- A threat of physical violence
- A threat of violence from hate-motivated mindset (i.e., racism, homophobia, etc.)
- Serious bodily harm
- Sexual abuse
- Any accusation of an illegal act, such as robbery or extortion.[17]

It's essential to create a culture where children and teens feel comfortable reporting issues without fear of retribution or non-action. When students know their environment is safe, and the adults around them are committed to preserving a positive culture free from bullying or abuse, they can focus on their learning and growth.

Rachel's Challenge

On April 20, 1999, Rachel Scott was one of twelve students who lost their lives at the hands of two classmates during a school shooting in Columbine High School in Columbine, Colorado. Following her death, many classmates shared stories of Rachel's kindness with her family, which prompted them to promote a positive climate in K-12 schools. Rachel's Challenge, the non-profit organization created in their daughter's memory, has since touched the lives of 25 million people with its mission of replacing bullying and violence with kindness and respect.[18]

Their program shares the story of Rachel: who she was and how she touched those around her during her seventeen years of life. It addresses the fears and anxieties that others may have and provides an opportunity for continued conversations to strengthen relationships. Rachel's Challenge has expanded beyond K-12 schools to include colleges and business with more than 1.5 million people involved in their program each year.[19]

Creating a culture of acceptance and inclusion is vital for success. We must bring these tough topics to the surface to ensure a safe, nurturing learning environment for everyone. Sharing the stories of others helps us recognize similarities in our own lives and strengthen empathy and compassion.

Online Trolls

When I first began sharing digital citizenship lessons with students, our goal was to keep students safe when they were visiting online websites and to be aware of online "trolls" who might appear in chat windows. Ten years later, I am still reminding students of trolls, but I'm discovering their prevalence has invaded virtually every online platform available. They are no longer random strangers; they might be people in the same room as you. Online negativity runs rampant, but trolling takes it to another level.

Sue Scheff and Melissa Schorr break down the characteristics of online trolls in *Shame Nation: The Global Epidemic of Online Hate*:

Classic Trolls

- Goal is to draw attention; unpleasant, but doesn't escalate
- Poke fun or rile up others about a particular topic

Recreational Trolls

- Annoying people who say hurtful things to you or about you

Criminal Trolls

- Intent to harm you, your family, your business[20]

Whether you categorize people as trolls or negative nellies, the message is still the same: We must take a stand against bullying and cyber harassment if we want to see positive change in this world. While the best advice is to ignore the trolls, there are times when you must act to stop the harassment. If you or someone you know is being bullied or harassed, tell someone immediately. Do not suffer in silence. Your life has value and you matter!

Sharing our stories of bullying might be a lifeline to someone else who is going through a similar experience but feels completely alone. Bystander Revolution showcases online videos created by teens, adults, and even television and movie personas, describing their personal experiences with bullying. Listening to those stories and learning firsthand from others what made their lives better provides hope and healing to those enduring the same challenges. Their website, BystanderRevolution.com, includes tips for dealing with bullying and toll-free hotlines where you can speak to someone about the issues you encounter.

Stems of strength and courage grow best in nutrient-rich soil with a stable root system as a foundation. There are many resources and programs available to create a culture of kindness in our homes, schools, workplaces, and communities. The key is keeping empathy and compassion in the forefront and following through with action when it's needed most.

Kindness Cultivator Spotlight

David James

#PeytonHeartProject
Twitter: @products4peyton
Instagram: products_for_peyton
Facebook: ThePeytonHeartProject
Website: thepeytonheartproject.org

David James, a teacher and coach at Lake Creek High School in Montgomery, Texas, knows the pain and trauma caused by bullying and the impact it can have on children. His son, Peyton, ended his life at the age of thirteen.

A few months following Peyton's death, Jill Kubin and Sue Harris approached David about doing a hat drive in coordination with Emily's Hats for Hope, a charity created by Jill's daughter, Emily. They collected and donated more than five hundred hats in Peyton's name.

Later that year, they contacted David with a desire to raise awareness of suicide, mental health issues, and bullying. They wanted to take small, handmade hearts with a positive message attached and leave them where people could find them. This was the start of the #PeytonHeartProject.

Since its inception in 2015, Peyton's Hearts have been found in all fifty states and more than sixty-five countries throughout the world. Each heart is handmade by a volunteer with an attached note guiding recipients to the Peyton Heart Project website, thepeytonheartproject.org, which includes information about the project as well as additional ways people can participate. "Peyton is my biggest inspiration, " David says. "He had such a kind and giving soul. He always wanted to help others, donate what he could, and make the world a better place."

David also keeps Peyton's memory alive by taking personal days from teaching to share Peyton's story. In one school, they started an act of kindness club following his visit; in another, a student confessed to his teacher that he was having suicidal thoughts and was able to receive assistance. "If what you do helps even one person, then it is worth all the trouble."

If you or someone you know is in a crisis, talk to a friend or family member or contact The National Suicide Prevention Lifeline at 1-800-273-TALK (8255), which will connect you with the nearest crisis center in the US national network. You can also seek help online at suicidepreventionlifeline.org. For international support, visit iasp.info.

To learn more about David James' passion for
kindness, favorite kindness quotes, and more,
visit tamaraletter.com.

Points to Ponder

 Describe your root system of support. What keeps you planted when the winds of change occur?

Who are those in your personal learning network (PLN)? How do their strengths complement yours?

Have you ever been the target of a bully or bullied someone yourself? How did that experience contribute to the way you respond to others today?

Chapter 10

Spring Flourish

Carry out a random act of
kindness, with no expectation of
reward, safe in the knowledge
that one day someone might
do the same for you.

—Diana, Princess of Wales

One of my fondest memories from high school was being a member of SODA. The Student Organization for Developing Attitudes paired high school students with fourth-grade classes throughout our district to create and deliver character-based lessons and provide opportunities for student mentorship.

It was a rigorous process to be selected into SODA, complete with a written application and multiple interviews. I can still remember the morning the SODA team came into my tenth-grade math class, interrupting the teacher to ask me to stand, and handed me a sealed envelope with a formal invitation to join their organization. The room erupted in spontaneous applause as I gathered my books and backpack to follow the current members into our school auditorium filled with parents, friends, and relatives who were already in on the surprise announcement.

We took our seats as the ceremony began and, as our names were called, we walked across the stage to receive our official SODA pin, to be worn with pride as we performed our official duties throughout the year.

In a school with almost 1,400 students, only forty-three students were tapped into SODA that year. That's only 3 percent of the entire student body! To say it was an honor to join this group would be a grand understatement. One of the first things we received was our "SODA Challenges" for the upcoming year, written by a senior SODA member years before:

1. **Be an OUTSTANDING SODA**. Be a role model for those around you. The name of SODA carries a lot of respect. Make sure you have the respect as an individual.

2. **Keep your personal standards high and those of SODA just as high**. Don't ever let the name of SODA lose its credibility. If SODA as a group loses respect, then it also loses its effectiveness.

3. **Give each other support**. Nobody said SODA was easy, just worthwhile. SODA will become a second family for you. Remember, you are all part of the same group. Don't cause SODA to come apart at the seams by dividing yourselves. Stick together. SODA is an extremely fragile organization. Just as one's respectability can be ruined easily, the reputation that these and other former SODAs have built for the group can easily be destroyed in one year. Don't let it happen.

4. **Be effective in the classroom**. Your primary function is to serve as role models for fourth graders. Listen to their problems. Take an interest in them as people and enjoy a

good relationship with your SODA teachers. These things take work and time, as does any worthwhile endeavor. But once you establish yourselves as positive, helpful, and caring SODAs in the classroom and out, you will know a special satisfaction few things will give you.

5. **Be willing to learn even as you teach**. If you keep your mind on what you are doing, the experiences in SODA will provide you with a wealth of knowledge. You will learn things from your sponsors, other SODAs, and especially your fourth graders.[1]

Although I was only fifteen years old, I knew the importance of joining SODA. We committed to attending afternoon meetings and carving time in our schedules to plan lessons with our SODA partners that were then submitted to our club sponsor and classroom teachers for review. Whether it was reading a story about empathy or engaging in a collaborative activity of writing compliments on paper plates taped to students' backs, we knew our lessons of kindness, respect, and team-building were planting positive seeds in those we served.

We visited our assigned classroom twelve times a year. Our "All About Me" posters hung on the classroom walls, a visual reminder to students that their SODA was always there. Our first week was filled with introductions that included an official SODA mailbox, where students could write us letters and we would write them back. The words those sweet fourth graders poured into their letters could make your heart soar or break into a thousand pieces.

They trusted us, and we trusted them. We became friends to the outcasts and voices for the silent. We led by example. We helped support a culture of acceptance and provided advice for those who asked.

We were the spring flourish for generations to come.

KitKatKards

Sometimes a seed of kindness prospers when you least expect it. When my daughter, Katrina, was in sixth grade, she and I attended a Girl's Night Out event at Chickahominy Middle School. I was excited that she still wanted to include me in a school function, so I eagerly marked the date on my calendar to attend.

We were greeted by her guidance counselor, Alyssa Farling, and handed a flyer with various activities. How we chose to spend our time was up to us, but we were encouraged to do things together. The first session we attended showcased card-making, emphasizing the joys in using our talents to create things for others. By the end of the evening, my daughter was making plans to create her own card-making business.

Over the next week, I helped her create a long-term business plan, identifying costs for materials and price points for sales. My previous experience as an assistant manager of a retail store helped me guide my twelve-year-old with ideas for marketing, budgets, and business management. My husband and I became her first investors, lending her thirty dollars to purchase blank cards, scrapbook paper, word stamps, and colored stamp pads.

She created a website, kitkatkards.wordpress.com, and named her business KitKatKards, using the nickname her Pappy gave her as a baby. We even ordered business cards, so she could promote her business when she met with potential clients (namely, friends and neighbors). We shared a discussion about the importance of giving back to others, and she made the decision to donate 10 percent of her profits to St. Jude Children's Hospital in Memphis, Tennessee. She then set an official goal of earning one thousand dollars in one year.

Through the kindness of others who heard about her entrepreneurship, my daughter's business flourished. She quickly learned how to complete homework, engage in extracurricular activities, and still have time to create handmade cards. Each time she donated to St. Jude Children's Hospital, she received an acknowledgment of her contribution with a card, letter, or a small gift. The organization explained the various ways it would use her money, reminding her that she was part of its mission to cure childhood cancer.

In less than a year, she reached her goal of making one thousand dollars, donating one hundred dollars to charity. Three years later, she became a Kiva investor, crowdsourcing her money with others around the world to provide micro-loans for people in impoverished countries. Today she is a college student, focused on becoming a financial advisor, while giving back to her local community through mission projects, community outreach events, and sharing her time and talents.

It all began with one activity at school. Imagine the impact we can have on our youth by emphasizing different ways we can make the world a brighter place. It might take years for the seed to flourish, but when it does, its beauty is everlasting!

For more information on Kiva, visit kiva.org.

Kind Kids

It's important for us to recognize and acknowledge ways our own children show kindness too. During a winter storm, my oldest son, Daniel, stopped sledding on the hill with his siblings and cousins when he realized his neighbor wouldn't be able to walk through the snow to get her mail. Ten minutes later, without any prompting from an adult, he had a shovel in hand, creating a pathway along her driveway towards the mailbox.

In the spring, when he joined his dad on an overnight Ragnar race, he volunteered to use his Red Flyer wagon to carry items from strangers' campsites to their cars, which involved pulling weighted items up a steep hill. He also wears a memory bracelet with the name of a classmate who passed away suddenly in seventh grade, a fundraiser started by another classmate at his school. Although it happened more than two years ago, he still wears the bracelet every day. "It's important to remember him," Daniel told me. "His life mattered."

My youngest son, Caleb, shares my heart for empathy. If he's playing a board game with someone else, he will offer suggestions on how to win if they are losing. He will clean his room to surprise me or give me a hug when I get home from a long day at work. He even chooses to give away his own toys to others, especially those who might be less fortunate than him.

Katrina, my firstborn, shows kindness in quiet ways. She makes gifts for her friends, painting canvases with their favorite colors and inspirational quotes. She remembers to wish people "Happy Birthday" and freely gives compliments when people least expect them. She rocked her brothers when they were younger and helped her grandpa on multiple occasions to clean his house. She even watched her brothers in the summer, so I could write this book!

These are small examples of my children scattering kindness in the world, and I bet you could make a long list of the kindness you see in children too. From nieces and nephews to kids who live down the street, if you watch how they interact with others, you will see small seeds of kindness being planted each day!

Embedding Kindness

I first met Brandi Miller (@bmilla84), a first-grade teacher at Caldwell Elementary in Auburndale, Florida, during a *Teach Like a Pirate* (#tlap) Twitter chat. Her positivity immediately caught my eye, and I instantly felt a connection. Several months later, I noticed her request to connect with classrooms across the world as part of her Global Collaboration project, so I offered to represent the state of Virginia.

Brandi's project focused on a virtual game of "Mystery Letter," where classrooms connected via Google Hangouts, taking turns asking yes-no questions to guess the other class's hidden letter. This classroom activity provided young students an opportunity to practice their verbal communication as they used collaboration and critical thinking skills to solve the mystery.

At the end of the collaborative game, classes would ask additional questions to learn more about each other, noting similarities and differences. It was a great way to broaden the students' understanding of the world around them. As the conversation drew to a close, Brandi and her students would exchange a kindness challenge for the other class to complete, sharing the results of their kindness challenges through social media.

In one school year, Brandi and her students scattered kindness to all fifty states in the United States and globally to Canada, Australia, and Chile. In all, they completed more than one hundred virtual collaborations. Think about all those seeds of kindness scattered by those children across the world and the impact it might have on others to do the same. It's simply incredible!

When we connected with Brandi to represent the state of Virginia, her class challenged Anthony Whitaker's first-grade class at Mechanicsville Elementary School to write kind messages with sidewalk chalk around our school. Our students challenged hers to write a compliment for someone else on a Post-it note to brighten their day. They were small, easy-to-complete challenges that helped spread kindness throughout the school but also around the world, thanks to social media.

Brandi and her students also created a #kindnessbucketlist that they completed in less than a month. Her passion for kindness is truly contagious!

Melisa Hayes (@hayes_melissa), a second-grade teacher at Avery Elementary in Hilliard, Ohio, embeds kindness in her lessons by having one student take center stage, sitting in front of their whiteboard. While the student is facing away, classmates come to the board and write positive comments about him or her on the whiteboard, with Melisa capturing the finished result with a photograph for the student to receive. What an incredible way to bolster self-esteem while creating a magical moment that will remain for years to come!

To view Melisa Hayes' Kindness Project,
visit youtu.be/4u2JVdVKCLQ.

Mandy Ellis (@mandyellis), principal and author of *Lead with Literacy: A Pirate Leader's Guide to Developing a Culture of Readers*, allows students and teachers at her school to select a new book for their birthday, choosing from a bookshelf stocked with books in a variety of topics and reading levels. "Birthday books celebrate the love of reading and support our school vision of creating a culture of readers," Mandy explains. "When you gift a book, you are building a culture of reading and gifting the love of reading!"[2] It's another great way we can embed kindness and celebrate value in others.

Dream Big

Emphasizing kindness in our culture has a direct impact on morale. While not everyone can be kind every moment of every day (Trust me, I've tried and failed countless times!), making a conscious choice to keep kindness in the forefront can lead to a shift with positive results.

When I decided to expand my kindness initiative at school, I allowed myself to dream big. "What if . . ." was a constant sentence starter in my mind as I pondered the possibilities. What if I wrote a grant and got some extra funding? What if I could work with a class on kindness lessons all year? What if I could create a way for children to experience the joys of kindness in small and extravagant ways? What if those same children could share their experiences with others? What if those children could inspire the world?

About the same time that I was swirling with ideas of integrating kindness with classroom lessons, I came across a YouTube video of this precocious little boy who called himself "Kid President." Robby Novak and his brother-in-law Brad Montague were already a hit sensation online, their inspirational videos viewed by millions of people around the world. I couldn't get enough of this adorable little boy and his vibrant personality!

Created to counteract the negativity of the 2012 presidential race, eleven-year-old Robby Novak dressed in a suit and shared his opinions about life:

What if there were two paths? I want to be on the path that leads to awesome . . . What will you create to make the world awesome . . .? This is our time. We can make every day better for each other.[3]

In the exact moment I was brainstorming ideas to inspire children, a child in the world inspired me. If you haven't read their book, *Kid President's Guide to Being Awesome*, I highly recommend it. It will leave you with smiles and inspire you with dozens of ideas to change the world for good!

A Passion for Kindness

With a renewed excitement, I brainstormed ideas with Lori Cross, a fourth-grade teacher in my building, and together we wrote a grant proposal for A Passion for Kindness, a year-long kindness initiative that would include weekly lessons culminating in kindness passion projects at the end of the year. We requested funding from the Hanover Education Foundation (hefhanover.com) to purchase kindness-themed books, lesson materials, and activity supplies. Two months later, we were delighted to discover that our proposal was fully funded!

Lori and I used her no-break day—the day when her teammates had a planning period, but she did not—to provide kindness

lessons to her students, expanding upon the ones I had taught in SODA years ago. Our students customized kindness journals to document kind acts they saw or received, then designated more pages for kindnesses they shared. We watched videos. We worked in groups. We read books like *Ordinary Mary's Extraordinary Deed* by Emily Pearson and explored the concepts of multiplying kindness while analyzing rhyming patterns throughout the book.

Lori's class completed 255 acts of kindness during the two weeks before winter break and celebrated kindness by creating posters to display around the school. Demonstrating a bit of flower power, we even distributed colorful daisies to the adults in our building, thanking them for all the ways they made our school better.

Our lessons focused on kindness, but they included so much more. We emphasized social-emotional learning skills like mindfulness and social interaction. We explored tough topics like bullying and respect and found ways to align our lessons with instructional content so the loss of instructional time was kept to a minimum.

We made kindness a priority for our students, who, in turn, made it a priority for us.

For a comprehensive list of kindness-themed books for children and adults, visit tamaraletter.com.

Kindness Passion Projects

During Random Acts of Kindness week in mid-February, we introduced Kindness Passion Projects. Referencing Kid President and his challenge to "be a day maker,"[4] we discussed all the ways we had shared kindness throughout the year, with most of our RAKs being free.

"What if you had ten dollars? How could you be a day maker then?" I asked our class, as I held up a ten-dollar bill and presented their challenge. "In the next few months, you are going to be the change we need to see in the world. Each one of you will receive a ten-dollar bill to fund your project. Your only task is to spend all the money on someone else in our local community, then create a

presentation to share what you did. Your project starts today. Let's get started!"

The gasps of surprise and sounds of excited chatter were enough to be a day maker right there! Many of our students had never held a ten-dollar bill, much less been given the opportunity to design their own projects, spending money on someone else. There was so much joy when they realized we really were going to do this!

Our first task was to tackle a timeline, so everyone knew what was expected and when. We chose a date in May to hold a Kindness Share Fair when students would showcase their projects. Working backwards, we designated weeks for researching, planning, conferencing, implementation, and project design. Knowing time was a precious commodity, we taught our lessons during the language arts block or no-break days for curriculum alignment.

Once we had our timeline set, we started with the basics. Who would our students bless with kindness? Forming small groups, they identified people and organizations of interest, which we compiled into a master list. Neighbors. Teachers. Hospital workers. Animal shelters. Dance studios. We saw glimmers of our

students' passions as they chose their project recipients and started to dream big.

Research and Planning

Each student received a planning page to tape into their kindness journal, similar to a science investigation with space for project title, purpose, materials, procedure, results, and reflection. Students were given free rein to spend their money however they liked. Some wanted to give their recipient a $10 gift card. Others wanted to use their money for supplies to make something. Even more wanted to fill gift baskets with treats and surprises to make someone else smile.

As students started to research prices for items on their materials list, they were shocked to discover how *little* they could purchase with ten dollars. Many had to redesign their projects due to funding constraints. One boy wanted to give a fruit basket to a cafeteria worker, filled with pineapples, oranges, and strawberries. He discovered through his research that fruit prices fluctuate based on the season, with some fruits like bananas being much cheaper than other fruits on his list. He was shocked to see that fruits like watermelon weren't available all year.

The learning that took place during the research phase of these kindness projects exceeded any lesson Lori and I could have prepared from a textbook or worksheet. This was real. Relevant. Personalized. Students were sharing their insights with classmates with a low hum of activity around the room. They learned which retail stores charged more for certain items and practiced their addition and multiplication skills while figuring out how many items they could afford to purchase. Some students even got a crash course in state sales tax, a topic that wasn't even covered in their fourth-grade math curriculum.

Passion Project Planning Page

Student Name:

Title of Passion Project: Coffee for my bus driver

Materials Needed and Cost per Item:

Construction paper	Free at school
Markers	Free at school
10$ Giftcard to Starbucks	$10.00

Procedure: My mom is going to take me to Starbucks
We are going to buy the giftcard
I am going to make the card at school
I am going to give the card and the giftcard
to Mrs. Davis

The most striking outcome was the shift in our classroom dynamics. Students were helping one another with research. They were showing kindness in the words they used to encourage one another in their work. Class disruptions and behavior issues were non-existent during our project planning, and engagement was at an all-time high.

Kindness Conferences

Since my schedule provided flexible scheduling, I offered to meet with each student individually for a kindness conference while Lori continued with other lessons of the day. She could have easily completed this task during station rotations or using digital recording tools like Seesaw or Flipgrid, but I was available and willing to help.

Students sat with me on the sofa in our school's Innovation Lab and gave me an overview of their kindness passion projects. We worked together to include additional information, like an organization's address, then identified additional support they would need to complete their projects. Most of the students needed someone to drive them to the store. Some needed help delivering their projects to others. For those who were surprising neighbors, we shared a conversation about safety in numbers and following parents' rules for walking through their neighborhood.

Each student was given a parent permission form following their kindness conference. To send the ten dollars home with each student, we had to have a commitment from parents or guardians to assist with the project as designated. We gave each student a week to return the form, which included a yes/no box for parent help and a place for parent and student signatures. We encouraged those parents who could help to take photos of the child's act of kindness and to email them or send them in for the final display.

In an ideal world, every parent would be able to help, but we do not live in an ideal world. As parents ourselves, we understand the constraints families face on a daily basis. Time is a precious commodity, not only during the school day but at home as well. We reassured parents that we could adapt their children's projects if they weren't able to help outside of the school day. There was no pressure on the parents to complete this activity with, or for, their children. These were the children's projects, and, one way or another, their children would be able to participate in this lesson of generosity.

Projects and Calamity

Our timeline included spring break as the optimal week to put their kindness passion projects in motion. For students who needed to complete their projects during the school day, we did so the week they returned. For the next month, students worked on writing, editing, and creating project displays for the Kindness Share Fair in May.

With our grant funding, we purchased science fair display boards, and students created headings and information using Google Docs and Google Classroom to print and adhere to the boards. Students became editors for each other, double-checking for spelling and grammatical errors.

The weeks leading up to the Kindness Share Fair were filled with nervous anticipation of sharing their projects with an authentic audience. We discussed ways to engage others in conversations, reviewed mindfulness techniques, and remembered how to calm our feelings. The students also practiced answering questions with their classmates to strengthen their capacity for oral speaking.

Then my world crashed around me. Two weeks before our Kindness Share Fair, my mom was hospitalized for the last time.

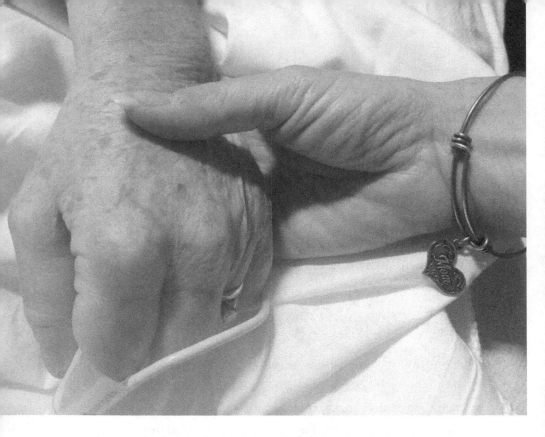

As I sat by her bedside with Bob, her husband of eighteen years and love of her life, time stood still. My world was filled with heart-beat monitors, breathing tubes, and beeping machines. Five days before the Kindness Share Fair, my mom took her final breath and passed away.

On the day of our Kindness Share Fair, when our students were excitedly sharing their projects with the world, I was making final arrangements for my mom's funeral. Beside me was a stack of handwritten cards and letters the students had created for my mom during her hospital stay; they arrived on my doorstep the morning after she was gone.

Some might say it was a shame their cards arrived so late, but I would disagree. It was perfect timing, arriving in the moment I needed them most. Those sweet sentiments from our students reminded me that *I* mattered to *them*. With colored hearts and pencil-made drawings, our students showed they understood the

true meaning of empathy and compassion. Our lessons of kindness had come full-circle. They made such an impact on me and my family that we displayed them at my mom's funeral.

I returned to school the Monday after the Kindness Share Fair and couldn't wait to see them again. But more calamity awaited on the horizon. Not even an hour after I arrived at school, Lori came into the Innovation Lab, talking on the phone with a panicked expression on her face. Her dad was in the hospital. She needed to leave. Immediately.

Without hesitation, I rearranged my schedule and taught her class the rest of the day. The students were excited to tell stories about the Kindness Share Fair and share the reflections they had written in their journals. It was a day filled with distraction, while Lori faced the same heartbreaking reality I had just experienced. Days later we learned that Lori's dad had passed away as well.

Perfect Timing

My Grandma Payne always used to say, "Everything happens for a reason." She loved this saying so much, we actually have Ecclesiastes 3:1 carved into her granite headstone. I'm not sure my limited understanding of life and death can process every single thing happening for a reason, but I do believe there are times in our lives when we walk through serendipity and find small moments of joy in the journey.

Losing my mother at such a pivotal time in our kindness projects was not a joyous experience—far from it! The kindness shown to me and my family during that time, however, was exceptional. Coworkers and friends fed my family for weeks when I didn't have the energy to even step into the kitchen. Strangers donated money to help with funeral and medical expenses. Cards and notes were sent reminding me that I was not alone in my grief. They were simple things done to bless me until I could get back to that place where I could pay it forward by blessing others again.

The following school year we expanded our kindness initiative to include two classrooms instead of one. Jennifer Madison, Lori Cross, and I became our own kindness triad, planning lessons together for a new group of students. We raised money for Jet Stream Jax as described in Chapter 3. We decorated placemats and wrapped silverware for Caritas as they provided meals for the homeless. We described our gratitude on a Padlet board, then shared with the world on Twitter using the hashtag #gratitudesnaps, a month-long gratitude movement led by Tara Martin and Tisha Richmond (@tishrich). With each act of kindness, we were reminded that kindness is always in season, always available, always the right thing to do.

Sharing kindness with others is always perfect timing.

To view the students' Kindness Passion
Projects, visit tamaraletter.com.

Night to Shine

From student passion projects to community celebrations, there are a multitude of ways to spotlight kindness. One of my favorite events is Night to Shine, an annual prom celebration created by Tim Tebow, former NFL football quarterback and current baseball player, geared for teens and adults with special needs. With no cost to guests, this event makes every attendee feel like the king or queen of the ball!

I was honored to attend Night to Shine as a surprise for my neighbor, Ashton Friedl, who was confined to a wheelchair. We had such a great time! Dinner was provided with several activities guests could participate in, from limo rides to photo booths to dancing on the dance floor. Our Night to Shine prom even included a shoeshine station for the boys! Each girl received a sparkling tiara to wear, and boys were given golden crowns. There

was a red-carpet arrival, complete with names announced over a loudspeaker and photographers on hand to capture the joyful moments.

What struck me most about this event was the unconditional love and acceptance of all the guests in attendance. There were so many smiles! Accommodations were made for those with limitations, and every guest had a designated buddy throughout the night. In a 2017 interview with Fox News, Tim Tebow described the prom in his own words:

It's my favorite night of the year, and we get to change so many lives. . . . It's so much more than life, because maybe for the first time, they realize that they're worth it. They realize that they're special. They realize that they're loved. There's not much more important than that.[5]

In its fourth year, Night to Shine celebrated more than 90,000 people with special needs. Wow! Talk about a spring flourish! Thanks to the Tim Tebow Foundation, sponsorship from 537 churches, and the support of 175,000 volunteers worldwide, this event shined with kindness and continues to grow each year.[6]

For more information about Night to Shine, visit timtebowfoundation.org/ ministries/night-to-shine.

Kindness Prom

What if there was a prom focused on kindness? In 2018, Instagram hosted a kindness-themed prom in partnership with Kindness.org to promote a passion for kindness with teen influencers. The star-studded event included actors and actresses from Disney Channel and Nickelodeon and hundreds of invited guests.

There was an anti-bullying balloon arch entrance, as well as activities like a make-your-own-crown table and positive affirmation wall. Hundreds of posts were shared on Instagram using the hashtag #kindnessprom in hopes that teenagers would be inspired to promote awareness of kindness and safety, both online and off.[7]

Attending prom is a milestone event for many teens, but some can't afford the costs associated with the occasion. Dresses alone can cost hundreds of dollars even before alterations! Rebecca Kirtman, a freshman at Nova High School in Davie, Florida, recognized this inequity and decided to transform intention to action with kindness. She launched a dress drive to collect prom dresses and accessories to distribute to others in need. The following year, she single-handedly collected and donated 250 formal dresses to teenagers in her local community.[8]

After Rebecca lost her life in a tragic car accident at the age of sixteen, her family continued her passion for kindness by creating Becca's Closet, a non-profit organization dedicated to providing opportunities for others. What began as a desire to help financially challenged teens attend prom now includes post-secondary educational scholarships to recognize those who share Becca's spirit of generosity.[9]

Empowering our youth to embrace their passions for serving others is securing our investment in a future filled with kindness cultivators. What spark of inspiration will you share today?

Kindness Cultivator Spotlight

Kelly Pace
Service Learning Projects
Twitter: @theoryofpace
Website: kellyapace.blogspot.com

"It's nice to be important, but it's more important to be nice." These inspiring words from Kelly Pace's childhood are words she shares with students in her IB English and Theory of Knowledge classes at Atlee High School in Mechanicsville, Virginia. As the CAS (Creativity, Activity, Service) coordinator for the IB Program, Kelly supervises full-diploma international baccalaureate candidates with month-long service projects.

Student projects demonstrate kindness, care, and commitment as students use their talents to add value to others' experiences. Their projects include making blankets for a homeless shelter, packing meals for Rise Against Hunger, leading canned food drives, and writing kind notes to hide around campus with the hashtag #AtleeLoves. They have also painted kindness rocks to hide at various elementary schools in the area.

Throughout the year, students strengthen skills of empathy and compassion as they partner with other classes in the district to lead as mentors. When students in the functional academics program altered the recipe for their cookie business, Kelly's students taste tested the cookies and provided feedback. Her students also wrote stories to read to their class.

Kelly's twelfth-grade students collaborated with a first-grade class using the digital tool Seesaw. The younger students read stories to the high school students, which led to discussions about the book and sharing photos, jokes, and more.

In addition to serving others, Kelly's students also showed gratitude to others by participating in "Lollipop Moments," inspired by Drew Dudley's TEDx presentation titled "Leading with Lollipops" (youtu.be/hVCBrkrFrBE). They gave lollipops to people who had made a difference in their lives and thanked them for what they had done.

Those seeds of kindness scattered even further when the Student Council Association adopted a school-wide initiative of Lollipop Moments. Each teacher gave every student in their first morning class a lollipop with four tags. One tag included something kind written about that student. The other three tags were blank, so students could pay it forward with compliments for others. "Some people judge themselves based on money, fame, or success," reflected Kelly. "The true success of a person is really how they treat others."

To learn more about Kelly Pace's passion for kindness, favorite kindness quotes, and more, visit tamaraletter.com.

Points to Ponder

 What moments of kindness do you recall from your childhood experiences?

How have you seen kindness flourish in your home, school, or community recently?

When have you experienced a "Lollipop Moment"? Were you the giver or recipient? What made that moment special in your life?

Chapter 11

Global Gardens

We make a living by what
we get, but we make a
life by what we give.

—Winston Churchill

F our years after I began my kindness journey with
forty acts of kindness, and two years after I became
a RAKtivist®, I had the privilege of visiting the Random Acts of
Kindness Foundation in Denver, Colorado, and meeting members
of their team: Rachelle Stubby, Brooke Jones, Kelsey Gryniewicz,
and Jeana Newsom.

They surprised me with several gifts, including bookmarks,
stickers, a poster, and two books about kindness. Their thoughtfulness touched my heart, as I wasn't expecting anything other than
the joy of finally meeting these kindness cultivators in person!

We walked to a local restaurant for lunch. As we sat down
to eat our meal, the conversation flowed freely and our shared

passion for kindness bubbled over our words. They apologized for the absence of their president, Gary Dixon, as he was attending the 2016 US Conference of Mayors to talk about kindness and compassion with a unique panel of like-minded kindness cultivators, including Lady Gaga, the Dalai Lama, and Philip Anschutz, an entrepreneur and philanthropist. Later, I researched the event to learn more. The words the Dalai Lama shared in his keynote mirrored my desire to spread kindness around the world:

Now the time has come that America should be the leading nation in the promotion of human compassion and love in order to become a compassionate world . . . I think in my lifetime we can achieve that. But effort must start now.[1]

How do we make kindness rise and scatter like those dandelion seeds of a childhood wish? We start now! Whether your kind act is small like a seed or as grand as a garden, it starts with *you.*

Imagine if each of us shared one positive post a day on our favorite social media platforms. Now imagine if we took one positive post from another person's page then shared it on our own feeds. Oh, my goodness! Talk about rising up and scattering seeds. We just might blanket the world with the beauty of kindness and inspiration!

This past year I made it my mission to connect with as many kindness cultivators as possible. I wanted to learn their stories and celebrate the joys of kindness. I posted tweets and retweets with the hashtag #passionforkindness and even created a Twitter list titled *Passion for Kindness* so I could filter my feed and see only posts from those who inspire me with kindness. On Facebook, I created a Passion for Kindness group where members can share acts of kindness and post their own inspirational thoughts. Now each morning when I wake up, my social media feeds are overflowing with positive, uplifting words and images.

To join the Passion for Kindness Facebook Group, visit facebook.com/groups/ passionforkindness.

Joyful Journeys in Hashtags

We all have wonderfully unique ways to scatter kindness and positivity to others. Sean Gaillard (@smgaillard), a principal at Lexington Middle School in Lexington, North Carolina, and author of *The Pepper Effect*, brightens the start of each workweek with his #CelebrateMonday and #TrendThePositive communities. Educators and district leaders spotlight positive things happening throughout their day on Twitter and include one or both of these hashtags, making it easy to share in the joy. Mondays have a brighter view, thanks to Sean's efforts in creating a virtual community focused on positivity!

Bethany Hill (@bethhill2829), a principal at Central Elementary in Cabot, Arkansas, also inspires with her #JoyfulLeaders community on Twitter. This hashtag spotlights the joyful things leaders experience as they shine for others in the world. Remember, you don't have to have a title to be a leader! If you are looking for a bright spot in your day, do a quick search of this hashtag, and I guarantee your spirits will soar.

As spotlighted in Chapter 1, I was blessed to connect with Akilah Ellison (@OrganicLeaderVB) on Twitter and discovered she worked only a few hours away! She was sharing her experiences as a #JoyAmbassador using her district-focused hashtag #VBHasJoy, and I instantly felt a connection. When I met her for the first time at her district's Joy Fair in February 2018, the warmth of her genuine smile and gentle spirit reminded me yet again of the positive impact we can have on others, even those we have never met before.

Many of the kindness cultivators mentioned in this book have their own kindness-themed hashtags that spotlight the joy in being kind to others. Whether it's a visual quote you might save to your mobile device or a blog post that spurs a moment of quiet reflection, you will create an incredible network of kindhearted leaders by following these people and hashtags:

- Roman Nowak (@NowakRo)–#bekindEDU
- Staci Erickson (@stacitoday)–#kindness180
- Melanie Korah (@melanie_korach)–#StarfishClub
- Kate Lapetino (@kcmgd31)–#FieldKindness
- Laurie McIntosh (@lauriemcintosh)–#TheKindClub and #KindnessCapes

When I share with my students that I use social media to connect with others in the world, they are often intrigued and ask lots of questions. "Who do you follow? How many people follow you? Are you famous and we don't know it?"

Their discussions make me laugh. Famous? What does that even mean? Who gets to decide when you've made the leap from ordinary to extraordinary? Do you need to be classified as famous to make a positive impact in the world around you? Posing these questions to students instantly draws them in as the conversation shifts from labels and status to value and purpose.

It's important to discuss social media with our students, namely the way we use various platforms to connect and share. Our students have instant access to the world daily, and it's our duty as teachers, parents, and community members to do all we can to guide them in using these online spaces to communicate in a positive, uplifting way.

Childhood Inspiration

Long before social media, I found inspiration from people on television. The small, color television that sat on our kitchen counter displayed only three local channels and a public broadcasting station. I can still remember adjusting the rabbit ear antennas to get better reception.

I learned lessons of empathy and kindness from the characters I watched on Sesame Street—adults with darker skin color speaking kindly to those who looked different from them and children who lived in apartments and sat on city stoops. I experienced diversity without anger and hate; in fact, I wasn't even aware of social and demographic disparity at that age. People were people. We were alike. We were different. We figured out a way to get along with one another.

Sesame Street addressed tough topics such as sadness, fear, and death. As a young child, I already had life experiences that would forever shape my perspectives of security and stability; Sesame Street was another safe place I could visit and find myself among friends. Today, nearly fifty years after its debut, Sesame Street still offers support for preschoolers and their parents, both on television and through its website at sesamestreet.org.

After Sesame Street, I would watch Mr. Rogers' Neighborhood, where Fred Rogers greeted me each day with a smile as he entered his home, changed from dress shoes to sneakers, and replaced his blazer with a red cardigan. When he spoke to the camera, it was as if he were in the room chatting with me, not as a child to be looked down upon, but as a person who had worth and value.

As I grew older and learned more about these childhood programs, and the efforts that went into keeping these shows on-air, I was humbled by the motivation and determination of many to bring empathy, compassion, and kindness into homes nationwide.

Joy Rising

Another television show that captured my interest was The Oprah Winfrey Show. In 2002, Oprah Winfrey visited a community in South Africa to bring Christmas joy to more than fifty thousand schoolchildren and orphans, many whose families had been killed by the AIDS epidemic. Following that visit, Oprah shared with her audience that students in South Africa were required to have uniforms to attend school and receive a formal education. Uniforms cost sixty dollars each, an exorbitant cost most could not afford. By sharing this need with her audience and those around the world, they collectively raised more than seven million dollars to cover the costs of school uniforms for these children.[2]

In 2004, Oprah Winfrey coined the phrase "joy rising" to describe the day she surprised her audience with kindness in the most extraordinary way.[3] Each person who arrived for that day's taping, 276 people total, received a wrapped box as the episode concluded. They were told that one lucky person would win a new car, identical to the ones given to guests earlier on the show. When Oprah told the guests to open their boxes, there were incredible outbursts of joy as every single person in the audience discovered a key to a new Pontiac G6. Amid the cries of excitement, Oprah shared in the jubilation, shouting, "You get a car! You get a car! Everybody gets a car!" In reflection of this monumental episode, Oprah Winfrey proclaimed the event "one of my all time, favorite, happiest moments ever!"[4]

Another annual tradition of The Oprah Winfrey Show was to spotlight several new products deemed "Oprah's Favorite Things," then surprise audience members with each of the products shown. In 2006, Oprah Winfrey wove kindness into the segment as she gave more than three hundred audience members Bank of America debit cards worth one thousand dollars and told them they had seven days to spend the money on a worthy cause. She provided each person with a Sony camcorder to capture the kindness they would share with others.[5]

The ripple effect of kindness continued as audience members shared their stories. One woman used her money to spearhead a fundraising campaign for a cancer-ridden man in her community that generated more than seventy thousand dollars and helped his family pay for medical bills and save their home from foreclosure.

Another audience member purchased four airline tickets for moms and dads to visit their sick children in a Hawaiian children's hospital. Go! Airlines then continued that spirit of kindness by donating an additional forty airline tickets for her mission. Countless stories of generosity shared on Oprah Winfrey's website continue to scatter seeds of inspiration for those who read their stories.[6]

Champion of Kindness

Another champion of kindness who made headlines in the talk show arena was Ellen DeGeneres who, at the time of this writing, continues to shine a light on kindness surprises with The Ellen DeGeneres Show. Using her comedic wit and brilliant smile, Ellen has created a fan base that might rival the likes of an NFL football team!

In 2016, she was honored by The People's Choice Awards to receive the Favorite Humanitarian Award for her generous contributions to schools, charities, and organizations that align with her passions, including survivors of natural disasters, abused and mistreated animals, and breast cancer research. She is also a fierce defender of diversity, vocally standing up for those who have experienced bullying throughout their lives. In all, she has donated more than fifty million dollars to make this world a better place since the start of her talk show in 2003.[7]

Ellen partnered with Cheerios in 2017 to spur a global garden of kindness, challenging others to perform One Million Acts of Good. Using the hashtags #GoodGoesRound and #OneMillionActsOfGood on Twitter, Facebook, and Instagram, kind words and actions could be shared across the globe. Ellen then brought select kindness cultivators on her show to share in a one-million-dollar reward for their kindness.[8]

While there are countless examples of Ellen's kindness and generosity, the one that resonates with me most is her quiet reminder at the end of each show: "Be kind to one another."[9] It's a simple call to action that reminds us of the importance of our actions each day.

Queen of People's Hearts

Sometimes the greatest acts of kindness are those that require no money, no words. More than thirty years ago, the world watched in disbelief as a princess shook the hand of an AIDS patient, neither wearing protective gloves. Dispelling the myth that the AIDS virus could be transmitted by casual contact, Princess Diana, the Princess of Wales in England, used empathy and compassion as her tools to spotlight kindness around the world.[10] According to her friend, singer and songwriter Elton John, "She gave voice to the voiceless and changed the way the world viewed the disease."[11]

Affectionately known as the "Queen of Hearts,"[12] Diana used her notoriety to draw attention to causes that connected people, creating a ripple effect that continues today. Her work with removing landmines, helping the homeless, and promoting the positive endeavors of youth inspired The Diana Award two years after her death in 1997. Since that time, more than forty-seven thousand young people around the world have received The Diana Award, which aims to support, celebrate, and empower youth changing the world in a variety of ways, no matter how big or small.[13]

Traveling Kindness

If you enjoy watching Netflix shows, you might be familiar with the name Leon Logothetis, the man who circumnavigated the globe relying on the kindness of others. In his show, *The Kindness Diaries*, he rode a vintage yellow motorcycle aptly named Kindness One, complete with side passenger cab, fueled and funded completely by the generosity of strangers he met among his travels. Whether it was a refilled tank of gas, a warm meal, or dry shelter, Leon's story of traveling kindnesses showcased for the world the impact complete strangers can have on someone in need.[14]

In the stories Leon shares on the show and in his books *The Kindness Diaries: One Man's Quest to Ignite Goodwill and Transform Lives Around the World* and *Live, Love, Explore: Discover the Way of the Traveler a Roadmap to the Life You Were Meant to Live*, you see a side of human nature that is often missed in the headlines. You witness hardworking men and women taking time out of their day to share in conversations, then offering Leon shelter and food. You discover people overcoming language barriers to offer a smile, a handshake, a hug. You see a homeless man sharing food from a friend and the clean clothes he received from a shelter before preparing a communal place to sleep outside with cardboard and worn blankets. Even the poorest of the poor show they have kindness to give.

"The act of giving and receiving is where the real magic of human connection occurs," Leon writes in *The Kindness Diaries*.[15]

Unbeknownst to some of the strangers sharing kindness with Leon, they were going to be recipients as well. Taking time to learn their story through conversations, Leon decided to bless them in a way that they could never imagine. For one family in Montenegro, he purchased a cow, so they could sell cheese and milk at the market. For a family in Delhi, he purchased a new rickshaw, and for a Cambodian woman and her son, isolated by disease and living in a makeshift shelter with sides of tin and loose boards for a roof, he built a new home.[16]

Leon's stories show the power of kindness to change the lives of many, including our own.

Local Celebrity

What makes celebrity kindness cultivators so powerful? Their humanity! Celebrities are real people with dreams, hopes, and ambitions, just like you and me. In 2009, students at my school wrote letters to Jason Mraz, two-time Grammy winner and singer-songwriter, asking if he would visit them. His song, "I'm Yours," had been playing on the radio for months, and students were shocked to learn that he was once a student at the same elementary school they were attending that year. Some students immediately pulled out their crayons, markers, and colored pencils to create cards and write letters, but a few students were skeptical of the chances that he would actually come for a visit. We reminded them, "If you never ask, the answer will always be no."

Months later, on a hot June day, our students' request was granted. Jason Mraz came to Mechanicsville Elementary School, walking down memory lane as he toured the campus and visited classrooms. Our students were mesmerized with wide-eyed wonder as Jason smiled, hugged, and answered questions, sitting near their desks and engaging in casual conversation.[17]

Then our students and teachers received an even grander surprise. Each classroom was led outside, where Jason Mraz performed a mini concert. As he played his guitar and sang songs from his latest album, I was brought to tears at his incredible kindness and generous spirit.

He answered our students' letters in a way they could have never imagined. He visited with them, sang with them, and shared his passion for kindness, love, and equity through his time and talent. He showed them that celebrities are real people, too, and emphasized the importance of making a positive difference in this world.

Jason Mraz continues to give back to our local community as he volunteers his time and talent, supporting the School of the Performing Arts in the Richmond Community (SPARC), which provides performing arts education to students with and without disabilities.[18] He also contributes to their annual LIVE ART performance, where he serves as Artistic Advisor.[19] On August 10, 2018, he surprised twenty SPARC students with the experience of a lifetime: to perform with him on *The Today Show* in New York City, New York.[20]

Kindness Outreach

Other celebrities stand out in my mind for their compassionate spirits and generosity. Danny Thomas, a radio, film, and television star who rose to fame years before I was born, founded St. Jude Children's Hospital, a state-of-the-art research and treatment facility dedicated to eradicating childhood cancer. As a former resident of Memphis, Tennessee, where St. Jude Children's Hospital is located, it was awe-inspiring to see the many ways this facility impacted our local community.

Although we lived in Memphis for only a few years, this hospital had an enormous impact on my passion for kindness. It was the first organization I knew that provided its services at no cost to patients and their families.

Think about that for a moment. In the United States, we are not guaranteed free healthcare. We have various insurance companies with a plethora of plans and prices. To provide insurance for a healthy individual is costly enough; to have a family member diagnosed with a life-altering condition like cancer makes those rates astronomical.

But Danny Thomas had a passion for kindness and an empathy for suffering children. He didn't feel it was fair for those families hurting the most to endure the crushing effect of financial strain. According to the St. Jude website, Thomas founded the American Lebanese Syrian Associated Charities (ALSAC) in 1957 to be the fundraising source for St. Jude Children's Hospital. Because of his vision and commitment to kindness, children who received services from St. Jude Children's Hospital were never charged a fee for their food, housing, treatment, or travel, a tradition that continues today.[21] This is one of the reasons my daughter chose it as her charity of choice when she created her card-making business as described in Chapter 10. She wanted to support an organization that supported children when they needed it most.

In 2002, a young student named Megan Smith sat in my third-grade classroom in Memphis, Tennessee. Sixteen years later, she joined the staff of St. Jude Children's Hospital, working as a pediatric oncology nurse. In reflecting about her firsthand experiences working at this benevolent hospital, she reminds us of the value of showing kindness in the workplace:

With nursing, I feel like kindness is part of the job description, and the definition changes from room to room. It could mean letting a parent vent about frustrations and just being a good listener. Or it could mean walking a family's laundry down to the washing machine, so the parents don't have to leave their child.

Small acts from coworkers are just as significant. A pump could be alarming while I am busy, and a coworker will jump up and take care of it, so it doesn't wake anyone up. It takes a team of people who understand the significance of kind acts, no matter how small they seem, to make what I do possible.[22]

Whether it's helping a coworker, assisting a friend, or surprising a stranger, we can cultivate kindness anywhere we go!

Tiny Tech Cafe

If you are a public school teacher in the United States, chances are high that you have spent your own money purchasing items needed for your classroom. Whether you grab an extra pack of pencils in the checkout line or fill up your shopping cart with supplies for a grand learning experience, your commitment to teaching and the materials needed to make it happen often supersede your monthly paycheck.

In 2016, there was a trending hashtag on Twitter that caught my eye: #StarbucksMyRoom. Flexible seating was starting to gain attention as educators were transforming their rooms to offer more opportunities for communication and collaboration. Intrigued, I scrolled through the feed to see countless photos of teachers turning areas of their classrooms into miniature coffee shops, complete with standing tables, bar stools, and cozy corners with comfortable seating.

As I looked at the plain, stark computer lab where I met with teachers to create and implement lessons, I wanted to do something similar, but knew I would never be able to afford the cost. I wanted a sofa! A bookshelf filled with current, relevant books to inspire teachers! A coffee bar and more. In a computer lab? Sure! Why not?

I created a GoFundMe Campaign and shared the link on my social media pages. I shared my vision for creating a collaborative space in our building and thought perhaps my closest of friends would support me with small donations. What happened next was astounding!

In the two weeks of my campaign, I had friends, coworkers, neighbors, local businesses, and complete strangers donate to my transformative space, which I named the Tiny Tech Cafe. One of our students' parents purchased a bookshelf from my wish list and built it over the weekend. Publishers donated books. Even my Zumba instructor, Toni Brunson, joined in the fun by surprising me with a brand-new Keurig!

Photo Credit: Lisa Zader, CapturedbytheLens.com

Our Tiny Tech Cafe remains today as a testimony to the kindness of others and the power of the phrase "better together." This space is used by many, and thanks to another Hanover Education Foundation grant, the room renovations have expanded to a completely transformed Innovation Lab for students and teachers, including flexible seating and equitable access for all.

When an act of kindness of one joins with the act of kindness of another, amazing things can happen!

The Ripple Effect

Another platform teachers use to secure items for their classroom needs is Donors Choose. Unlike GoFundMe, which processes monetary payments and disperses them to recipients (minus a service fee), Donors Choose allows donors the opportunity to choose a project to fund, then will put their donation towards the project as a whole. When the project is fully funded, the requested items are then sent to the recipient's school to be used for their classroom.

The concept of random donors choosing educational projects to fund was the brainchild of history teacher Charles Best in 2000. Creating a simple website, his coworkers posted the first eleven requests. Eighteen years later, Donors Choose has eighty team members with more than six hundred thousand project requests fully funded.[23]

For teachers, Donors Choose can be like a dream come true. With classroom teachers spending hundreds of dollars from their own salaries to provide additional resources and supplies for their classrooms, a gift from a benefactor is priceless. With 79 percent of all public schools in the United States represented by a project request on this site, the impact on students' learning and achievement is widespread.[23]

On March 26, 2018, those dreams *did* come true. Ripple (@ripple), a company created to "establish an Internet of Value: a world where money can move like information,"[24] donated $29 million dollars to fully fund *every project* listed on the Donors Choose website. That's more than thirty-five thousand educational experiences now possible through the generosity of one company! The news went viral on Twitter, Facebook, and Instagram using the hashtag #BestSchoolDay and was even showcased on late night TV.[25]

What is your ripple effect in this world? How do you use your talents and gifts to benefit the world around you? Could you join forces with someone to make a broader impact with your passions? Together we can cover the world with global gardens of kindness!

Kindness Cultivator Spotlight

Laurie McIntosh
#KindnessCapes and #TheKindClub
Twitter: @lauriesmcintosh
Website: mrsmacskindergarten.blogspot.ca

One person who has firsthand experience of Ellen DeGeneres' kindness is Laurie McIntosh, a kindergarten teacher in Lethbridge, Alberta, Canada. In 2015, she won tickets to attend a taping of the show, during which she was invited to the stage to play a fast-paced guessing game called Heads Up. She won the game and was rewarded with a trip to Las Vegas, Nevada. What Laurie didn't know, however, was the very next week she would be a scheduled guest on Ellen's show, receiving a new car and each of the "12 Days of Giveaways" prizes.

To see her kindness surprise moment, visit ellentube.com/video/a-new-car-for-a-sweet-couple.html.

Laurie weaves stories she sees on The Ellen DeGeneres Show into her instructional lessons, showing students different ways we can be kind to one another. She even transforms her students into champions for kindness.

"It takes courage to be kind when no one else is," explains Laurie. "Because superheroes are the most courageous people of all in a five-year-old's mind, the capes they wear become a visual representation that they will be Kindness Superheroes for the day." With this mindset, #KindnessCapes was born, with each student in Laurie's class donning a brightly colored cape to take walks together performing acts of kindness in their school and surrounding community.

Laurie shares the most important aspect of the students' #KindnessCapes missions: reflection at the end. "We always designate time to reflect through words, art, or stories ... how we felt during the walk, what we observed, and how we think other people feel about our mission. The reflection helps us to focus on the true meaning behind what we do and how kindness makes us feel."

In addition to #KindnessCapes missions, Laurie and her friend Valerie Hu (@valeriehu6) created The Kind Club, a global club of kindness through which students complete monthly kindness challenges. Teachers can register their class by sending an email to thekindclub2016@gmail.com and join in the fun by sharing acts of kindness online using the hashtag #TheKindClub.

To learn more about Laurie McIntosh's passion for kindness, favorite kindness quotes, and more, visit tamaraletter.com.

Points to Ponder

 Which social media platforms do you use the most. Why?

 Who are the Kindness Cultivators you are connected to in person and digitally? How have they impacted your own Passion for Kindness?

How can we create these "joy rising" moments in our classrooms, work spaces, homes, and communities?

Chapter 12

Be the Good

Go into the world and
do well. But more
importantly, go into the
world and do good.

—Minor Myers, Jr.

Kindness inspiration is everywhere if you choose to see life through the lens of empathy and compassion. From quotes pinned to Pinterest boards to small moments gone viral on YouTube, our ability to see kindness in this world is merely a keyboard click or cell phone tap away.

Even if we choose to disconnect and unplug, kindness can still be found in our daily interactions with those around us. It can be as fleeting as the spark of light in a morning sunrise, or it can linger like the swirl of a cool breeze on a hot, summer day, wrapping us in contentment and peace.

What is it about kindness that speaks to our souls? What experiences connect our hearts and minds to scatter kindness in the lives of others? How are seeds of kindness planted in you?

When I was seventeen years old, I saw the theatrical production of *Les Misérables* for the first time at The Mosque Theater in Richmond, Virginia.[1] Although I had never read the book written by Victor Hugo, I was swept away by the musical score and dramatic storyline of the play. There was a scene in the prologue that caught my breath. The main character, Jean Valjean, is released from prison on parole after nineteen years of incarceration. His crime? Stealing a loaf of bread to save his sister's son from starvation.

No longer a prisoner in a jail cell, he discovers that he is prisoner of the public, deemed an outcast, with hateful onlookers that regard him with disdain. A kind bishop takes in Valjean, but the former prisoner cannot break away from his old habits and steals silver from the bishop. He is quickly apprehended, and the police demand that he be thrown back into jail.

Suddenly, a plot twist. (Spoiler alert! If you haven't seen *Les Misérables*, you might want to skip a page ahead!) The bishop shows exceptional kindness by not only pretending that he gave Valjean the silver but adding two silver candlesticks to the loot. The police release him, and the bishop uses this as a teachable moment of empathy and compassion to give him a call to action through song:

"You must use this precious silver to become an honest man. . . . God has raised you out of darkness, I have saved your soul for God!"[2]

As the musical continues, Jean Valjean is indeed a saved man, who completes countless acts of kindness from that single act of kindness shown by the bishop so many years before.

I had to ask myself, Would I have done that? Would I have given another person such grace, even after they blatantly stole from me and lied about it? Could I have found a way not only to forgive their atrocities, but to offer even more? What would be the cost to me?

I grappled with these questions for years. I know the horrors of jealousy, hate, and spitefulness. I have held tightly to the woes of pain, anger, and repulsion to the point where the mental blisters of anguish burst open. The healing salve of unconditional kindness and grace is also something I know well. I have been humbled by the unexpected and the undeserved. I have learned how to recognize those small moments of good and hold them close, transforming them from words and thoughts to actions and deeds, choosing to shift my perspective by cultivating kindness in others.

I am reminded of the power we share when we work together for good, choosing to look past our differences and focus instead on our commonalities. It is in those moments we become the good we want to see in the world.

RAK Mob for Rosa's

In 2015, I attended the International Society for Technology in Education (ISTE) Conference in Philadelphia, Pennsylvania. Prior to the conference, there was a video circulating on YouTube about a man who opened a pizza shop in the same city, called Rosa's Fresh Pizza, with a unique pay-it-forward idea of feeding the homeless from the generosity of others. For the cost of one dollar, people could purchase a single Post-it to stick to the walls of the restaurant. Homeless people who needed a warm meal could come into the restaurant, take a Post-it from the wall, and redeem it for one slice of pizza at no cost.

To view the Rosa's Fresh Pizza video,
visit youtu.be/brzjelCclt0.

Intrigued, I started pondering the idea of raising money to take to Philadelphia to purchase Post-it notes at this restaurant. About the same time, I saw a Tweet from Ashley Hurley (@ashleyhhurley), who was also attending the ISTE Conference, inviting others to join in the fun. It would be a RAK Mob of Kindness!

I couldn't wait to get started! I posted a plea on Facebook with friends and family donating money and headed to ISTE with a pack of Post-it notes in my pockets and enough money to provide 125 meals for the homeless.

When I walked into the restaurant, I was overwhelmed by the colorful walls, completely covered in Post-it notes! It was an incredible sight to see, especially knowing that all the squares represented more than a slice of pizza. They represented kindness. Value. Hope.

There were letters and notes also attached to the walls, words of gratitude from those who had been the recipients of such kindness, as well as inspirational notes from strangers. Hundreds of dollars were donated that day, thanks to the generosity of many. As an added bonus of joy, I was able to meet many members of my EduMatch® PLN in person: Sarah Thomas (@sarahdateechur), Ashley Hurley (@ashleyhhurley), Tara Linney (@TaraLinney), Rodney Turner (@TechyTurner), and more.[3]

The RAK Mob at Rosa's was a fun way to start our conference and make a positive difference in the world. When we work together to show kindness to others, our impact is endless!

Better Together

There are times in our lives when we need the help of others to make our dreams come true. Born with cerebral palsy, Sepp Shirey loved the game of football, despite his physical challenges playing the game. He never let his limitations define him, playing football through his school years. Inspired by one of his favorite football players, Tim Tebow, he proudly wore the number fifteen on his football jersey, a shout-out to Tebow's Wish 15 Foundation.[4]

During Senior Night, Sepp Shirey stood on the sidelines watching his teammates play in one of the final games of their high school career. Little did anyone know, the night would end with triumphant jubilation from the power of kindness, collaboration, and perseverance.

Atlee High School's Head Coach, Matt Gray, made the decision to put Sepp in the game with a plan to carry the ball a few yards before being tackled by two-hand touch. Just a few steps into the play, everything changed. Taesean Crutchfield, a linebacker on the opposing team from Varina High School, saw Sepp's movements and caught his eye as he ran down the field. "I just wanted him to score because I knew it would be a good feeling for him," Taesean said.[5]

Taesean's teammates quickly followed his lead, clapping and cheering for Sepp as he ran a total of eighty yards—more than he had ever run before—to cross the end zone for a touchdown. The crowd on both sides of the field erupted with joy, with many adults and students in tears over the incredible acts of selflessness and determination.

The story was shared on our local news stations and quickly caught the attention of others. With more than 230,000 views on YouTube,[6] this story of kindness quickly went viral, being told on major news networks, including ESPN[7] and *The Today Show*![8]

Sepp Shirey is from my hometown. Taesean Crutchfield lives in a neighboring district. Either of these boys could live in your hometown too! There is nothing more exciting than seeing people helping one another reach their milestone moments. The people in the stadium that day, and those who have watched the video since, have seen the true definition of *better together*.

What many people may not know, however, are the hardships that have plagued Taesean most of his life. "Fourteen-year-old Taesean? He probably wouldn't have even wanted to be on the field," Taesean reflects, "Fourteen-year-old Taesean was selfish, thought about himself, didn't really have feelings. It just had to change."[9]

Despite being placed under house arrest and serving time in juvenile detention for mishaps years ago, a journey similar to Jean Valjean in *Les Misérables*, Taesean, now a senior in high school, sees his life through a different lens, which led to the monumental act of kindness he shared with Sepp Shirey on the football field. In reflecting about his journey, Taesean recalls, "There are times I could have died, and there's times stuff could have happened and gone terribly wrong, but God has my role for me. Everything I do,

I take advantage of because most people don't get second chances. When you do, it's a blessing."[10]

Every life has value and purpose. It's our mission to help people see the incredible potential they have inside to be the good for others.

Kindness Cultivator Spotlight

Melinda Forward

Revolution Through 1,000 Thank Yous
Twitter: @Melinda_Forward
Websites: TheKindnessClub.net

What if you could revolutionize someone's journey with a simple "thank you"? This is what happened to Melinda Forward, a former French teacher in Albuquerque, New Mexico, who discovered a card of gratitude from a former student tucked away in her bookcase. "When I found this note, I found hope. I realized that I had made a difference. I realized that I had changed her world."

That moment sparked a radical idea: to challenge an entire student body to write one thousand thank you letters or cards in ten days or less. Carving out even ten minutes a week could shift perspectives from negative to positive, with gratitude as the catalyst. Melinda shared her idea during a TEDxABQED presentation in 2017 (youtu.be/yDZK0QGZNkk), explaining what makes this concept so powerful. "The 'why' touches the heart. It's lasting. It's tangible. It's something you can keep forever."

Inspired by a Kindness Club meeting during lunch at her school, Melinda founded Kindness Club International, where she serves as the creative director and the school culture turnaround specialist. She now cultivates kindness through training, tools, and support, to help schools organize and implement kindness culture builders. "It's not always easy being an activist for kindness. No matter what, never give up on your mission to make the world a better place."

To learn more about Melinda Forward's passion
for kindness, favorite kindness quotes, and more,
visit tamaraletter.com.

Call to Action

When I began my kindness journey, I had no idea how far and wide it would spread. I wanted to celebrate my fortieth birthday in a creative way and thought doing kind things for others would be a unique experience for such a milestone. What I discovered in the following years was that every act of kindness I completed was a seed planted for someone else. With every story I shared, the seeds scattered.

I believe we all have the potential to be kindness cultivators. You are probably one already! Even if you don't embrace kindness as your primary mission in life, at some point you are going to experience it. Someone is going to reach out to you, whether it's something simple like a smile or a door held open or a surprise of generosity that pulls you through. Are you going to allow that kindness to bloom, or will you push that seed back into the soil?

Every interaction you have, whether it's at school, work, home, or in the midst of your travels, is an opportunity to plant seeds in others.

Seeds of empathy.

Seeds of compassion.

Seeds of kindness.

You're making your mark on this world in small but meaningful ways; you might not even realize all the good you have shared with others. Even if you haven't considered the endless impact of your words and actions, the fact remains that you are a gardener. A cultivator. You are planting and sowing seeds in others that will eventually sprout and grow. Your seeds will give way to other forms of kindness, which have the potential for even more seeds to scatter, take root, and sprout. You have the power to create a global garden of kindness, all from one simple seed you took the time to sow.

That's the beauty of kindness; it doesn't have boundaries. It isn't limited to race, religion, gender, or location. It can be small. It can be grandiose. It's a characteristic of the soul, a universal language of the heart. It's a mindset you either embrace, or you don't.

It's a choice.

We can make a difference for so many people in our world. Our children. Our friends. Coworkers. Neighbors. Strangers. We have the opportunity to change someone's life.

Every.

Single.

Day.

I hope you catch a glimmer of the positive impact you have created in the world around you. That's what a passion for kindness is really about: realizing your role in making this world a better place for others, then having the courage to be kind again and again and again.

I have a passion for kindness, and I believe you do too. We share this driving force that compels us to do more.

To be the good. To spark the light. To become a catalyst of change. Together we can be the good we want to see in the world.

One seed at a time.

@woodard_julie

Points to Ponder

 In what ways has this book inspired you to share kindness with others?

 How will you share your message of positivity to inspire the world?

What are three things you will commit to doing this week to be the good?

Kindness Campaigns and Organizations

Nothing great was ever
achieved without enthusiasm.

—Ralph Waldo Emerson

*T*hroughout the year, there are many kindness celebrations, uniting like-minded kindness cultivators in their mission to make this world a better place. While some are hosted by organizations, others are social campaigns promoted on social media platforms like Facebook, Twitter, and Instagram. Visit the websites below to learn more and discover ways you can connect with others across the country (And the world!) to enjoy the enthusiasm of kindness. Resources are shared in chronological order based on dates of their events.

The Great Kindness Challenge

thegreatkindnesschallenge.com

End of January, lasts one week

The Great Kindness Challenge, a kindness outreach promoted by Kids for Peace, provides a school or family checklist of acts of kindness you can complete during their designated week of kindness. They also offer opportunities to become a Kindness Ambassador or a Kindness Certified School District.

Night to Shine

timtebowfoundation.org/ministries/night-to-shine

Early February, yearly

Sponsored by the Tim Tebow Foundation, the Night to Shine prom celebrates individuals with special needs while showcasing God's love for them. This yearly event is free of charge to guests who attend, thanks to church partnerships and foundation grants. Visit their website for more information.

National Random Acts of Kindness Day

February 17 each year

Celebrated in several countries, this national day of kindness is an opportunity for communities to share in the joy of kindness!

RAK Week

randomactsofkindness.org

Middle of February, lasts one week

#RAKweek followed by two-digit or four-digit year (e.g. #RAKweek2018)

A week-long celebration of kindness promoted by The Random Acts of Kindness Foundation. Visit their website and search "RAK Week" for previous posts of RAK Week activities and ideas.

Pay it Forward Day (PIFD)

payitforwardday.com

April 28 each year

People in more than eighty countries celebrate kindness on Pay it Forward Day with a goal of inspiring more than ten million acts of kindness around the world.

Annual Melee of Kindness (AMOK)

randomacts.org/amok

June/July, lasts four weeks

Sponsored by Random Acts, randomacts.org/, this global celebration of kindness has extended past twenty-four hours to now include an entire month of kindness fun. Follow the hashtag #AMOK or #AMOKRA to learn more.

International Day of Friendship

un.org/en/events/friendshipday

July 30 each year

Created in 2011, The International Day of Friendship strengthens empathy and compassion between people, countries, and cultures emphasizing peaceful activities between communities and promoting an "international understanding and respect for diversity."

Random Acts of Kindness Day–New Zealand

rak.co.nz

September 1 each year

Created in 2005, this first national kindness celebration is embraced by individuals, schools, churches, and local businesses. They even offer downloadable RAK cards you can use to accompany your acts of kindness!

Socktober

soulpancake.com/socktober

The month of October, every year

Sparked by a passion that "the smallest acts of kindness . . . can make a big difference in the lives of our neighbors who are homeless," Socktober is a yearly sock drive promoted by SoulPancake, Kid President, and Brad Montague.

World Kindness Day

theworldkindnessmovement.org

November 13, every year

Created in 1997, the World Kindness Movement provides an opportunity for kindness to be spotlighted worldwide. This organization now includes representatives from over twenty-eight nations, including the United States. The first World Kindness Day was celebrated November 13, 1998, and continues each year.

RAK Friday

The Friday after U.S. Thanksgiving Day

#RAKFriday (often followed by two digit year; e.g. #RAKFriday18)

Instead of focusing on Black Friday shopping, share your passion for kindness by deliberately showing kindness to others on this busiest shopping day of the year!

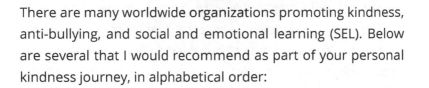

There are many worldwide organizations promoting kindness, anti-bullying, and social and emotional learning (SEL). Below are several that I would recommend as part of your personal kindness journey, in alphabetical order:

All for Good

allforgood.org

A great way to show kindness is volunteering your time to help others. All for Good provides links to local organizations and unique volunteering opportunities.

Becca's Closet

beccascloset.org

Becca's Closet continues the legacy of Rebecca Kirtman to provide prom dresses to high school girls in financial need. Groups can create their own chapter or discover a drop-off location nearby. Becca's Closet also offers scholarships and volunteer opportunities.

CASEL

casel.org

The Collaborative for Academic, Social, and Emotional Learning (CASEL) provides research and resources to "make evidence-based social and emotional learning (SEL) an integral part of education from preschool to high school."

Empatico

empatico.org

Empatico is a free, web-based tool that also connects classrooms around the world. In partnership with The KIND Foundation, this platform began as a vision of Daniel Lubetzky, the son of a Holocaust survivor, to promote empathy and build bridges between people. Currently available for students ages seven to eleven, Empatico provides younger students the opportunity to embrace their natural curiosities while learning more about the world around them.

Kids for Peace

kidsforpeaceglobal.org

Promoting worldwide peace and kindness, the Kids for Peace organization sponsors fundraising campaigns and initiatives to make the world a better place. Visit their website for more information on their peace pledge or becoming a peacebuilder.

Kindness.org

kindness.org

Looking to join in the fun of sharing kindness around the world? Kindness.org spotlights photos and stories of kind acts, and provides opportunities for people to get involved with kindness research as Citizen Scientists. Funded by the NEON Foundation, this non-profit organization connects the world with their #choosekindness hashtag and opt-in email list.

Kiva

kiva.org

This non-profit organization provides crowdsourced micro loans for individuals in developing countries with a minimum twenty-five-dollar donation. Teachers can access Kiva U Toolkits for use in the classroom at kiva.org/kivau/toolkits.

Making Caring Common

mcc.gse.harvard.edu

Making Caring Common is a project created at the Harvard Graduate School of Education in Cambridge, Massachusetts, which serves this mission: To create a culture of caring that promotes community responsibility and justice in this world. They provide resources and various kindness campaigns and initiatives throughout the year. You can also register your school as a Caring School and sign up to receive monthly newsletters filled with inspiration.

Montague Workshop Resources

montagueworkshop.com/resources

If you love the Kid President videos on YouTube, this is a must-have collection of resources shared by Brad Montague, the creator of Kid President. Focused on kindness, joy, and encouragement, lessons include downloadable printables, videos, and extension activities for technology integration.

Rachel's Challenge

rachelschallenge.org

The first victim of the Columbine school shooting in 1999, Rachel Scott's passion for kindness continues today through Rachel's Challenge, a non-profit school program to bring awareness of bullying and social-emotional relationships, while creating a ripple effect of kindness in school culture.

Random Acts

randomacts.org

Random Acts is a non-profit organization committed to celebrating and promoting kindness acts that range from everyday acts of kindness to community-based projects that benefit a multitude of people. Some of their programs include the Crisis Support Network, Class Act, Kindness Heroes, and Juneau Year of Kindness. Random Acts also promotes the Annual Melee of Kindness (AMOK) each year.

The KIND Foundation

kindsnacks.com/our-mission

Created in 2004 with the mission to "do the kind thing for your body, your taste buds, and the world," KIND created The KIND Foundation to celebrate and actively promote kind acts in the world. Its website includes information about its mission, special projects, and printable resources.

The Random Acts of Kindness Foundation

randomactsofkindness.org

Founded in 1995, this Colorado-based nonprofit organization promotes kindness through a multitude of resources and programs. Educators can access free resources and lesson plans on their website specifically designed for kindergarten through eighth grade, including UK lesson plans from foundation stage through Year Six. The Random Acts of Kindness Foundation also offers monthly calendars of kindness ideas, videos, stories, and more. You can apply online to be a RAKtivist® and join its Facebook group, a growing community of like-minded kindness cultivators sharing the ways they are showing kindness in the world.

Yale Center for Emotional Intelligence

ei.yale.edu

This group promotes compassion by providing information and resources about emotional intelligence focused on scientific research. Connect with them to learn more about the RULER approach and other ways to promote compassion in schools, workplaces, communities, and more.

Notes

Chapter 1

1. Joy Kirr, *Shift This!: How to Implement Gradual Changes for MASSIVE Impact in Your Classroom* (San Diego: Dave Burgess Consulting, 2017), 62-72.
2. Tara Martin, "Gratitude First," *Tara Martin* (blog), September 13, 2017, tarammartin.com/gratitudefirst.
3. Sue Scheff and Melissa Schorr, *Shame Nation: The Global Epidemic of Online Hate* (Napierville: Sourcebooks, 2017), 109.

Chapter 2

1. Nelson Mandela, *Long Walk to Freedom: The Autobiography of Nelson Mandela* (New York: Little, Brown and Company, 2008), 622.
2. Dave Burgess, *Teach Like a Pirate: Increase Student Engagement, Boost Your Creativity, and Transform Your Life as an Educator* (San Diego: Dave Burgess Consulting, 2012), 153-160.

Chapter 3

1. Jennifer Barnum, January 7, 2013, 11:23 p.m., comment on Celebrate Kindness, "New Beginnings: Act 1," celebratekindness. wordpress.com/2013/01/06/new-beginnings-act-1.
2. Jennifer Casa-Todd, *Social LEADia: Moving Students from Digital Citizenship to Digital Leadership* (San Diego: Dave Burgess Consulting, 2017), 197.
3. George Couros, "Same Message, Different Delivery," *The Principal of Change* (blog) November 5, 2017, georgecouros.ca/blog/archives/7833.

4. Barbara Gruener, "Peaceful Hearts Playground," *The Corner on Character* (blog), February 1, 2018, corneroncharacter.blogspot.com/2018/02/peaceful-hearts-playground.html.

5. RVA Rocks! VA Official Page, Facebook, facebook.com/groups/RVARocks/.

6. Rob Cardwell, "Building Better Minds: Kindness Rocks at Mechanicsville Elementary," March 14, 2018, WTVR Channel 6 News, wtvr.com/2018/03/14/kindness-rocks-bbm/.

7. Sara McCloskey, "Elementary school students reach out to Parkland with Kindness Rocks," March 6, 2018, WRIC Channel 8 News, wric.com/community/elementary-school-students-reach-out-to-parkland-with-kindness-rocks_20180326073953573/1078324371.

Chapter 4

1. Dave Burgess, *Teach Like a Pirate: Increase Student Engagement, Boost Your Creativity, and Transform Your Life as an Educator* (San Diego: Dave Burgess Consulting, 2012), 158.

2. Dana, July 20, 2014, comment on Celebrate Kindness, "Random Act of Kindness–My 100th RAK Blog Post," celebratekindness.wordpress.com/2014/04/17/random-acts-of-kindness-my-100th-rak-blog-post.

3. "The Science of Kindness," The Random Acts of Kindness Foundation, accessed July 3, 2018, randomactsofkindness.org/the-science-of-kindness.

4. Eva Ritvo, MD, "The Neuroscience of Giving: Proof that Helping Others Helps You," *Psychology Today*, April 24, 2014, psychologytoday.com/us/blog/vitality/201404/the-neuroscience-giving.

5. "The Mirror Neuron Revolution: Explaining What Makes Humans Social," *Scientific American*, accessed November 2, 2018, scientificamerican.com/article/the-mirror-neuron-revolut/.

6. Mary Daily, "Neuroscientist Marco Iacoboni on how mirror neurons teach us to be human," *UCLA Newsroom*, October 19, 2016, newsroom.ucla.edu/stories/ marco-iacoboni-mirror-neurons.

7. Jennifer Casa-Todd, *Social LEADia: Moving Students from Digital Citizenship to Digital Leadership* (San Diego: Dave Burgess Consulting, 2017), 29.

8. Steve Annear, "People Are Carrying Out 318 Random Acts of Kindness Across Boston," *Boston*, February 25, 2014, bostonmagazine.com/news/2014/02/25/ cathy-ogrady-acts-of-kindness-boston.

Chapter 5

1. Tamara Letter, "Secret Sisters," *Celebrate Kindness* (blog), February 8, 2015, celebratekindness.wordpress. com/2015/02/08/secret-sisters.

2. Erica Lantz, "Secret Sisters," Kind World radio program, December 20, 2016, wbur.org/kindworld/2016/12/20/ kind-world-33-secret-sisters.

Chapter 6

1. "National School Lunch Program," United States Department of Agriculture, accessed November 2, 2018, ers.usda.gov/topics/ food-nutrition-assistance/child-nutrition-programs/national- school-lunch-program.aspx.

2. "Key Statistics & Graphs: Food Security Status of U.S. Households in 2017," United States Department of Agriculture, accessed November 2, 2018, ers.usda.gov/topics/food-nutrition- assistance/food-security-in-the-us/key-statistics-graphics.aspx.

3. "Definitions of Food Security: Ranges of Food Security and Food Insecurity," United States Department of Agriculture, accessed November 2, 2018, ers.usda.gov/topics/

food-nutrition-assistance/food-security-in-the-us/definitions-of-food-security.aspx.

4. Sam McLeod, "Maslow's Hierarchy of Need," *Simply Psychology*, accessed July 25, 2018, simplypsychology.org/maslow.html.

5. Ricky Pradhan, "Application of Bloom's Taxonomy in E-Learning," XLPro, March 24, 2018, playxlpro.com/application-of-blooms-taxonomy-in-e-learning/.

6. Zach Parr, telephone conversation with author, July 25, 2018.

7. Sheryl Sandberg and Adam Grant, *Option B: Facing Adversity, Building Resilience, and Finding Joy* (New York: Alfred A Knopf, 2017), 55.

8. Elisabeth Kubler-Ross, *On Death and Dying: What the Dying Have to Teach Doctors, Nurses, Clergy, and Their Own Families* (New York: Scribner, 1969), 134.

9. Tara Martin, *Be REAL: Educate from the Heart* (San Diego: Dave Burgess Consulting, 2018), 104.

10. Allyson Apsey, *The Path to Serendipity: Discover the Gifts Along Life's Journey* (San Diego: Dave Burgess Consulting, 2018), 61.

Chapter 7

1. Bridget Murray Law, "Seared in Our Memories," *American Psychological Association*, 42, no. 8 (2011), 60, accessed on August 8, 2018, apa.org/monitor/2011/09/memories.aspx.

2. Tim Carman, "The Dirt on Hanover Tomatoes, Well-loved in Central Virginia," *The Washington Post*, August 16, 2011, washingtonpost.com/lifestyle/food/the-dirt-on-hanover-tomatoes-well-loved-in-central-virginia/2011/08/11/gIQAHgnHJJ_story.html.

3. "What Is Compassion," *Greater Good Magazine*, accessed on July 11, 2018, greatergood.berkeley.edu/topic/compassion/definition.

4. Ibid.

5. Tara Cousineau, PhD, *The Kindness Cure: How the Science of Compassion Can Heal Your Heart and Your World* (Oakland: New Harbinger Publications, 2018), 39.

6. "Suspended Coffee: How It Works," website, accessed on May 25, 2018, suspendedcoffees.com/how-it-works/.

7. Mayra Cuevas, "Thanks Au Lait: 750 Pay It Forward at Starbucks Location," *CNN*, August 24, 2014, cnn.com/2014/08/21/us/starbucks-pay-it-forward-chain/index.html.

8. Shelley Burgess and Beth Houf, *Lead Like a PIRATE: Make School Amazing for Your Students and Staff* (San Diego: Dave Burgess Consulting, 2017), 151.

9. Michele Borba, *UnSelfie: Why Empathetic Kids Succeed in our All-About-Me World* (New York: Touchstone, 2016), 31.

10. Houston Kraft, "Episode 2–Houston Kraft," July 31, 2018, in *Character Speaks*, produced by Barbara Gruener, podcast, MP3 audio, 29:05, itunes.apple.com/us/podcast/character-speaks-with-barbara-gruener/id1415337962?mt=2.

11. "Character Strong," website, accessed August 3, 2018, characterstrong.com.

12. Houston Kraft, "Episode 2–Houston Kraft," July 31, 2018, in *Character Speaks*, produced by Barbara Gruener, podcast, MP3 audio, 29:05, itunes.apple.com/us/podcast/character-speaks-with-barbara-gruener/id1415337962?mt=2.

13. "A Ballsy Sense of Tumor," website, accessed July 25, 2018, aballsysenseoftumor.com.

14. Justin Birckbichler, "PCL10: How to Talk to a Cancer Patient," *A Ballsy Sense of Tumor* (blog), August 5, 2017, https://aballsysenseoftumor.com/how-to-talk-to-a-cancer-patient/.

Chapter 8

1. Betty Smith, *A Tree Grows in Brooklyn* (New York: Harper & Row, 1947), inside cover.
2. Smith, 9.
3. Jimmy Casas, *Culturize: Every Student. Every Day. Whatever It Takes.* (San Diego: Dave Burgess Consulting, 2017), 7.
4. "What Is SEL?" CASEL, accessed June 20, 2018, casel.org/what-is-sel/.
5. "What Is RULER?" Yale Center for Emotional Intelligence, accessed June 20, 2018, ei.yale.edu/ruler/ruler-overview/.
6. Debbie Arco, personal conversation with author, July 25, 2018.
7. Bryan Skavnak, "Be the Nice Kid," Happy Golf Starts Here, accessed July 15, 2018, thehappiestgolfer.com/story-bethenicekid/.
8. "Christian's Buddy Bench," website, accessed July 18, 2018, buddybench.org.
9. April Roberts, email conversation with author, July 17, 2018.

Chapter 9

1. "Can You Eat the Yellow Dandelion Flower or Just The Green Stem?" SFGate, accessed July 15, 2018, homeguides.sfgate.com/can-eat-yellow-dandelion-flower-just-green-stem-75344.html.
2. "Dandelion" University of California Agriculture & Natural Resources, January 2018, ipm.ucanr.edu/PMG/PESTNOTES/pn7469.html.
3. "Tragic Events," Fred Rogers Productions, accessed May 8, 2018, fredrogers.org/parents/special-challenges/tragic-events.php.
4. Lizzie Velasquez, *Dare to Be Kind: How Extraordinary Compassion Can Transform Our World* (New York: Hachette, 2017), 15.

5. "Facts About Bullying," U.S. Department of Health and Human Services, accessed July 10, 2018, stopbullying.gov/media/facts/index.html.

6. "Suicide Rates in the United States Continue to Increase," Centers for Disease Control and Prevention, accessed July 10, 2018, cdc.gov/nchs/products/databriefs/db309.htm.

7. "Facts About Bullying," U.S. Department of Health and Human Services, accessed July 10, 2018, stopbullying.gov/media/facts/index.html.

8. Christine Elgersma, "It's Not Cyberbullying, But ..." Common Sense Media, October 1, 2018, commonsensemedia.org/blog/its-not-cyberbullying-but.

9. Anna Costanza Baldry, David P. Farrington, and Anna Sorrentino, "School Bullying and Cyberbullying Among Boys and Girls: Roles and Overlap," *Journal of Aggression, Maltreatment, & Trauma* 26, no. 9 (July 2017): 937, doi.org/10.1080/10926771.2017.1330793.

10. Ibid.

11. "Mobile Kids: The Parent, The Child, and The Smartphone," The Nielsen Company, February 28, 2017, https://www.nielsen.com/us/en/insights/news/2017/mobile-kids--the-parent-the-child-and-the-smartphone.html.

12. Christine Elgersma, "It's Not Cyberbullying, But ..." Common Sense Media, October 1, 2018, commonsensemedia.org/blog/its-not-cyberbullying-but.

13. Lizzie Velasquez, *Dare to Be Kind: How Extraordinary Compassion Can Transform Our World* (New York: Hachette, 2017), 37.

14. Ronald E. Riggio, Ph.D., "Are You an Easy Target for Bullies?" *Psychology Today*, January 3, 2013, psychologytoday.com/us/blog/cutting-edge-leadership/201301/are-you-easy-target-bullies.

15. Jennifer Casa-Todd, *Social LEADia: Moving Students from Digital Citizenship to Digital Leadership* (San Diego: Dave Burgess Consulting, 2017), 194.

16. Lizzie Velasquez, *Dare to Be Kind: How Extraordinary Compassion Can Transform Our World* (New York: Hachette, 2017), 21.

17. "Respond to Bullying," U.S. Department of Health and Human Services, accessed July 10, 2018, stopbullying.gov/respond/on-the-spot/index.html.

18. "Rachel's Challenge," website, accessed July 15, 2018, rachelschallenge.org.

19. Ibid.

20. Sue Scheff, Melissa Schorr, *Shame Nation: The Global Epidemic of Online Hate* (Naperville: Sourcebooks, 2017), 159.

Chapter 10

1. "SODA Challenges," written communication provided to author, 1988.

2. Mandy Ellis, written communication, November 5, 2018.

3. "Video: A Pep Talk from Kid President to You," Soul Pancake, accessed July 31, 2018, soulpancake.com/portfolio_page/kidpresident/.

4. Brad Montague and Robby Novak, *Kid President's Guide to Being Awesome*, (New York: Harper Collins Children's Books, 2016), 115.

5. Caleb Parke, "Tim Tebow's 'Night to Shine' Celebrates 90,000 People with Special Needs Worldwide," *Fox News*, February 14, 2017, foxnews.com/us/2018/02/09/tim-tebows-night-to-shine-celebrates-90000-people-with-special-needs-worldwide.html.

6. Ibid.

7. Caterina Andreano "Instagram Pays It Forward by Throwing a 'Kindness' Prom for Teen Influencers," *ABC News–Good Morning America*, May 7, 2018,

abcnews.go.com/GMA/Culture/instagram-pays-forward-throwing-kindness-prom-teen-influencers/story?id=54972167.

8. "Becca's Closet," website, accessed August 1, 2018, beccascloset.org/about.

9. "Becca's Closet," website, accessed August 1, 2018, beccascloset.org/scholarships.

Chapter 11

1. Brian Eason, "Dalai Lama, Lady Gaga Urge Kindness in Indy," *Indy Star*, June 26, 2016, indystar.com/story/news/politics/2016/06/26/dalai-lama-lady-gaga-urge-kindness-indy/86247112.

2. "ChristmasKindness Inspiration," OWN: Oprah Winfrey Network, accessed July 20, 2018, oprah.com/oprahshow/christmaskindness-inspiration/all.

3. "Oprah's Ultimate Car Giveaway/Oprah's Life Class/Oprah Winfrey Network," YouTube video, October 15, 2011, youtu.be/8CAscBCdaQg.

4. Ibid.

5. "Paying it Forward," OWN: Oprah Winfrey Network, accessed July 20, 2018, oprah.com/spirit/paying-it-forward.

6. Ibid.

7. "Ellen Wins the People's Choice Humanitarian Award!/TheEllenShow" YouTube video, January 6, 2016, youtu.be/atNiYtCTcPc.

8. "Ellen and Cheerios Celebrate One Million Acts of Good With $1 Million!" EllenTube, Season 15 Episode 94, accessed July 20, 2018, ellentube.com/video/ellen-and-cheerios-celebrate-one-million-acts-of-good-with-1-million.html.

9. Ellen DeGeneres Facebook page, EllenTV video, accessed July 20, 2018, facebook.com/ellentv/videos/10154020282567240/.

10. Danny Boyle, "Prince Harry Invokes Images of Princess Diana Holding Hands of Dying AIDS Patient as He Warns of HIV Complacency Threat," *The Telegraph*, July 21, 2016.

11. Ibid.

12. Bill Smith, "Princess Diana still Britain's 'Queen of Hearts' 20 Years after Death," dpa International, August 16, 2017, dpa-international.com/topic/princess-diana-still-britain-queen-hearts-20-years-death-170827-99-795810.

13. "Diana's Legacy," website, accessed July 20, 2018, dianaslegacy.co.uk/dianas-legacy.

14. "The Kindness Diaries," Netflix television show, accessed July 25, 2018, netflix.com/title/80156137.

15. Leon Logothetis, *The Kindness Diaries: One Man's Quest to Ignite Goodwill and Transform Lives Around the World* (White Plains: Reader's Digest, 2015), 5.

16. Logothetis, 92-96, 124-130, 182-186.

17. "Jason Mraz Visits His Former Elementary School in Mechanicsville, Virginia/RichmondTimesDispatchVideo," YouTube video, June 4, 2010, youtu.be/j8HEjAyGEO8.

18. "SPARC History," SPARC, accessed on November 3, 2018, sparcrichmond.org/history/.

19. "LIVE ART," SPARC, accessed on November 3, 2018, sparcrichmond.org/liveart/.

20. "Watch Jason Mraz Sing, 'Have It All' Live on TODAY," *Today Online*, August 10, 2018, youtu.be/o1FXsvnFHtE.

21. "How St. Jude Began," St. Jude, accessed July 30, 2018, stjude.org/about-st-jude/history/how-we-began.html.

22. Megan Smith, written communication, July 20, 2018.

23. "About Us," DonorsChoose, accessed July 28, 2018, donorschoose.org/about.

24. Monica Long, "Ripple and Its Executives Proud to Support America's Public Schools with $29 Million XRP Donation to DonorsChoose.org," Ripple, March 27, 2018, ripple.com/insights/ripple-executives-proud-support-americas-public-schools-29-million-xrp-donation-donorschoose-org/.

25. Stephen Burke, "#BestSchoolDay2018: Every Project Funded!" The DonorsChoose Blog, March 27, 2018, donorschoose.org/blog/best-school-day-2018/.

Chapter 12

1. *Les Misérables*, music by Claude-Michel Schönberg, English lyrics by Herbert Kretzmer, The Mosque, Richmond, VA, February 6, 1990.

2. Norman Large, *Valjean Arrested, Valjean Forgiven*, recorded 1987, track 2 on *Les Misérables (Original Broadway Cast Recording)*, The Verve Music Group, compact disc.

3. Tamara Letter, "RAK Mob at Rosa's," Celebrate Kindness (blog), June 28, 2015, celebratekindness.wordpress.com/2015/06/28/rak-mob-at-rosas/.

4. Lane Casadonte, "The Story Behind Sepp Shirey's Inspirational Touchdown Run," WTVR Channel 6 News, November 2, 2017, wtvr.com/2017/11/02/the-story-behind-sepp-shireys-inspirational-touchdown-run.

5. Ibid.

6. "Atlee High School–Sepp Shirey–TD Run/KGMediaUS," YouTube video, October 27, 2017, youtu.be/kHKtpn6lMsc.

7. "Football Player with Cerebral Palsy Scores 80-yard Touchdown," ESPN, accessed August 1, 2018, espn.com/video/clip?id=21300405.

8. "See Fellow Players Help a High Schooler with Cerebral Palsy Score a Touchdown," *TODAY Online*, November 2, 2017, today.com/video/see-fellow-players-help-a-high-schooler-with-cerebral-palsy-score-a-touchdown-1087285827782.

9. Lane Casadonte, "Blessed with a Second Chance, Varina Senior Taesean Crutchfield Shines for His Football Family," WTVR Channel 6 News, October 25, 2018, wtvr.com/2018/10/25/blessed-with-a-second-chance-varina-senior-taesean-crutchfield-shines-for-his-football-family.

Acknowledgments

This book began as God's quiet whisper on my heart to share my kindness journey with the world. It is an honor to serve as a witness, showcasing the power of kindness and love.

A special thanks to Dave and Shelley Burgess, for taking a chance on this first-time author and guiding me from idle thoughts, blog posts, Twitter chats, and more to create a legacy of kindness for others. You are dream makers, wish granters, and two of the kindest people I know.

To Erin Casey, Mariana Lenox, and your incredible team, thank you for your talent, patience, and expertise throughout the publication process. You inspire me in all you do!

To Genesis Kohler, thank you for perfectly capturing my heart with the front cover design. You make dandelions beautiful in every way!

To Julie Woodard, whose sketches dance across the pages of this book, thank you for your kindness and generosity as you bless us with your talent and passion. To view more of Julie's sketchnotes, visit smore.com/fmdva.

To my mom, Dottie "Grammy" Shaver, and dad, Ken "Pappy" Payne, thank you for giving me life when you had barely begun your own. I hope my journey has made you proud.

To Laura "Grandma" Payne, thank you for being the rock of stability in my life. Although you are gone, you are never forgotten.

To my husband, Richard, and my children, Katrina, Daniel, and Caleb, thank you for your enthusiasm and understanding during this busy season of writing. From early mornings to late nights and everything in between, you sacrificed your "Mommy Moments" so I could pursue my dream of becoming an author. You are loved to the moon and back.

To Lisa Zader, my forever friend and ZTA Big Sis, thank you for decades of friendship and a lifetime of joy. You inspire me always with your kind, generous, loving spirit and incredible photography skills. ZLAM! Seek the noblest!

To Dick "Grandpa" Letter, thank you for the endless Saturday morning breakfasts, homemade treats for the Tiny Tech Cafe, and always asking how my book is progressing. Your kindness has helped me push through the tough times.

To my coworkers and administrative teams, thank you for allowing me the privilege of working with you and your students. Each day you remind me why I wanted to be a teacher so many years ago!

To Lori Cross, Jennifer Madison, and Maureen Ambrose, thank you for sharing my passion for kindness, inviting me to work with you and your students each month, and being my beta readers when I first began writing this book. Your encouragement helps me strive for greatness.

To my boss, Debbie Arco, and my entire ITRT team at Hanover County Public Schools, thank you for being the best cheerleaders a gal could ever have. I am humbled to be a part of the amazing work you do each and every day!

To The Local Cup, thank you for always welcoming me with a warm smile, a comfy place to write, and perfectly crafted Dulce de Leche.

To my extended family and faithful friends, thank you for sharing in my joy and taking an interest in my passion for kindness. For those who have spent hours listening to me ramble on about this book, you will have a special place in my heart forever!

To my Twitter PLN, I started to list you by name then realized there weren't enough pages to thank you all. Your kind words and thoughtful responses through Voxer chats, private messages, retweets, podcasts, blog comments, and more have transformed me as an educator. I am who I am today because of the small seeds you have planted in me. Let's keep growing together!

To the Kindness Cultivators, Secret Sisters, and inspirational individuals spotlighted throughout this book, thank you for granting me the privilege of sharing your stories with the world. I am honored to know you and share a small space in your kindness journey.

To all my students from 1997 to now, thank you for the countless hugs, endless laughter, and showing me the rewards of being a teacher. It has been a complete joy to watch you learn, grow, and succeed.

To anyone who has ever been called "the nice kid", this book celebrates you! Be strong and courageous. Keep inspiring, even when you think nobody notices.

They do!

Invite Tamara Letter to your school, business, or social event.

Tamara is an energizing and passionate presenter who inspires and empowers others to strive for greatness in all they do. She has shared her expertise as a keynote speaker, conference presenter, and professional development instructor as well as through podcast interviews, magazine articles, and video conferencing connections. Her presentations are engaging and interactive, spotlighting a variety of topics including:

 Cultivate Kindness with Technology Integration

 Bring Joy to the Classroom with Passion Projects

 From Teacher to Author: Finding Your Voice and Sharing with the World

 Your Story Matters! An Educator's Guide to Sharing on Social Media and Beyond

 From Heartache to Hope: Embracing Joy in the Journey

If you would like to invite Tamara to your school, business, or social event, connect with her below:

@tamaraletter

tamaraletter.com

celebratekindness@gmail.com

More from Dave Burgess Consulting, Inc.

Since 2012, DBCI has been publishing books that inspire and equip educators to be their best. For more information on our DBCI titles or to purchase bulk orders for your school, district, or book study, visit **DaveBurgessConsulting.com/DBCBooks**.

More from the Like a PIRATE Series

Teach Like a PIRATE by Dave Burgess

Explore Like a Pirate by Michael Matera

Learn Like a Pirate by Paul Solarz

Play Like a Pirate by Quinn Rollins

Run Like a Pirate by Adam Welcome

Lead Like a PIRATE Series

Lead Like a PIRATE by Shelley Burgess and Beth Houf

Balance Like a Pirate by Jessica Cabeen, Jessica Johnson, and Sarah Johnson

Lead beyond Your Title by Nili Bartley

Lead with Culture by Jay Billy

Lead with Literacy by Mandy Ellis

Leadership & School Culture

Culturize by Jimmy Casas

Escaping the School Leader's Dunk Tank by Rebecca Coda and Rick Jetter

From Teacher to Leader by Starr Sackstein

The Innovator's Mindset by George Couros

Kids Deserve It! by Todd Nesloney and Adam Welcome

Let Them Speak by Rebecca Coda and Rick Jetter

The Limitless School by Abe Hege and Adam Dovico

The Pepper Effect by Sean Gaillard

The Principled Principal by Jeffrey Zoul and
  Anthony McConnell

The Secret Solution by Todd Whitaker, Sam Miller, and
  Ryan Donlan

Start. Right. Now. by Todd Whitaker, Jeffrey Zoul, and
  Jimmy Casas

Stop. Right. Now. by Jimmy Casas and Jeffrey Zoul

They Call Me "Mr. De" by Frank DeAngelis

Unmapped Potential by Julie Hasson and Missy Lennard

Your School Rocks by Ryan McLane and Eric Lowe

Technology & Tools

50 Things You Can Do with Google Classroom by Alice Keeler
  and Libbi Miller

50 Things to Go Further with Google Classroom by Alice Keeler
  and Libbi Miller

140 Twitter Tips for Educators by Brad Currie, Billy Krakower,
  and Scott Rocco

Code Breaker by Brian Aspinall

Creatively Productive by Lisa Johnson

Google Apps for Littles by Christine Pinto and Alice Keeler

Master the Media by Julie Smith

Shake Up Learning by Kasey Bell

Social LEADia by Jennifer Casa-Todd

Teaching Math with Google Apps by Alice Keeler and
  Diana Herrington

Teaching Methods & Materials

All 4s and 5s by Andrew Sharos

The Classroom Chef by John Stevens and Matt Vaudrey

Ditch That Homework by Matt Miller and Alice Keeler

Ditch That Textbook by Matt Miller

Educated by Design by Michael Cohen

The EduProtocol Field Guide by Marlena Hebern and Jon Corippo

Instant Relevance by Denis Sheeran

LAUNCH by John Spencer and A.J. Juliani

Make Learning Magical by Tisha Richmond

Pure Genius by Don Wettrick

Shift This! by Joy Kirr

Spark Learning by Ramsey Musallam

Sparks in the Dark by Travis Crowder and Todd Nesloney

Table Talk Math by John Stevens

The Wild Card by Hope and Wade King

The Writing on the Classroom Wall by Steve Wyborney

Inspiration, Professional Growth, & Personal Development

Be REAL by Tara Martin

Be the One for Kids by Ryan Sheehy

The EduNinja Mindset by Jennifer Burdis

The Four O'Clock Faculty by Rich Czyz

How Much Water Do We Have? by Pete and Kris Nunweiler

P Is for Pirate by Dave and Shelley Burgess

The Path to Serendipity by Allyson Apsey

Sanctuaries by Dan Tricarico

Shattering the Perfect Teacher Myth by Aaron Hogan

Stories from Webb by Todd Nesloney

Talk to Me by Kim Bearden

The Zen Teacher by Dan Tricarico

Children's Books

Dolphins in Trees by Aaron Polansky

The Princes of Serendip by Allyson Apsey

About the Author

Tamara Letter is an enthusiastic educator who began her teaching career in 1997. Since then, she has taught students in Las Vegas, Nevada, Memphis, Tennessee, Staunton, Virginia, and now serves students and staff in her hometown of Mechanicsville, Virginia.

Throughout her journey as elementary teacher, differentiation specialist, technology integrator, and kindness cultivator, Tamara has inspired many with her creative and innovative learning experiences. She received her bachelor's degree in Interdisciplinary Studies from Radford University in 1994 and her master's degree in Educational Leadership from James Madison University in 2006, which sparked an interest in instructional coaching and sharing her expertise at local, state, and international events.

In 2014, Tamara shared her kindness journey publicly as an Ignite presenter for the International Society for Technology in Education (ISTE) Conference in Atlanta, Georgia. Following that event, she received funding from the Hanover Education Foundation and Renee's Cheerios to bring her passion for kindness into the classroom with unique, relevant, and empowering lessons that include service-learning components. She enjoys showcasing student Kindness Passion Projects each year at her school's annual Kindness Share Fair.

In 2018, Tamara received an R.E.B. Award for Teaching Excellence from the R.E.B. Foundation and was named 2019 Teacher of the Year for Mechanicsville Elementary School. She also serves as the Social Media Chairperson for the Virginia Society for Technology in Education (VSTE) Conference.

Tamara continues to inspire others as a motivational speaker, spotlighting stories from her website, tamaraletter.com. Her greatest accomplishment is being a mom to her three children, Katrina, Daniel, and Caleb.

Connect with Tamara on your favorite
social media sites below:

@tamaraletter

@tamaraletter

facebook.com/groups/passionforkindness

CPSIA information can be obtained
at www.ICGtesting.com
Printed in the USA
JSHW020905120120
3522JS00003B/9